White Servitude
in Maryland
1634–1820

Eugene Irving McCormac, Ph.D.

HERITAGE BOOKS
2010

HERITAGE BOOKS
AN IMPRINT OF HERITAGE BOOKS, INC.

Books, CDs, and more—Worldwide

For our listing of thousands of titles see our website
at
www.HeritageBooks.com

A Facsimile Reprint
Published 2010 by
HERITAGE BOOKS, INC.
Publishing Division
100 Railroad Ave. #104
Westminster, Maryland 21157

New Material Copyright © 2002 Heritage Books, Inc.

Originally published
Johns Hopkins Press
Baltimore, Maryland
1904

— Publisher's Notice —
In reprints such as this, it is often not possible to remove blemishes from the original. We feel the contents of this book warrant its reissue despite these blemishes and hope you will agree and read it with pleasure.

International Standard Book Numbers
Paperbound: 978-1-58549-754-6
Clothbound: 978-0-7884-8510-7

CONTENTS.

Chapter		Page
I.	INTRODUCTION	7
II.	THE EARLY LAND SYSTEM IN MARYLAND	11
III.	NUMBER AND ECONOMIC IMPORTANCE	27
IV.	INDENTURE AND "CUSTOM OF THE COUNTRY"	37
V.	FUGITIVE SERVANTS	48
VI.	STATUS OF SERVANTS AND FREEDMEN	60
VII.	SERVANT MILITIA	80
VIII.	CONVICTS	92
	CONCLUSION	107

WHITE SERVITUDE IN MARYLAND

CHAPTER I.

INTRODUCTION.

White servitude as it existed in Maryland and the other colonies was only a modified form of the system of apprenticeship which had been in vogue in England for several centuries preceding. The wide use of this system of labor during the fifteenth and sixteenth centuries accounts in a great measure for the readiness with which persons in later years entered into a contract of servitude in order to reach the New World. Not only were persons regularly bound out to masters for the purpose of learning various trades, but it was customary in the early part of the sixteenth century for parents of all classes to apprentice their children to strangers at an early age.[1] Used at first for training tradesmen and domestics, the system was extended to agricultural laborers during the reign of Elizabeth. The condition of the laborer had become so reduced by the debase-

---

[1] The following contemporary account illustrates how common this custom was in the first part of the sixteenth century. "The want of affection in the English is strongly manifest toward their children; for after having kept them at home till they arrive at the age of 7 or 9 years at the utmost, they put them out, both males and females, to hard service in the houses of other people, binding them generally for another 7 or 9 years. And these are called apprentices, and during that time they perform all the most menial offices; and few are born who are exempted from this fate, for every one, however rich he may be, sends away his children into the houses of others, whilst he, in return, receives those of strangers into his own."—Italian Relation of England, Camden Society, 1847.

ment of the currency, the change from tillage to sheep-farming and the numerous enclosures of land during the preceding reigns [2] that vagrancy and crime were met with on every hand. Attempts were made to better the conditions by compulsory apprentice laws [3] and by forced contributions for the poor.[4] Work was to be provided for those who were able to do it, and relief for those who were not. Poor children were to be trained for some trade and the idle were to be punished. In the reign of James I. the statutes of Elizabeth for binding children were made use of for sending them to the plantations.[5] But statutory remedies failed to afford adequate relief, and, in spite of the general prosperity during Elizabeth's reign, the condition of the poorer classes was deplorable.[6] In the latter part of the reign and during that of James, attempts were made to relieve England of her surplus population by founding colonies in America. The early expeditions were ill-planned and ill-managed. No systematic methods were adopted for supplying the plantations with laborers and failure was inevitable. In order to maintain a permanent and profitable settlement, a constant supply of laborers from the mother country was indispensable, but without pecuniary assistance the poor of Europe were unable to emigrate.

Various schemes were proposed for promoting emigration, the most successful of which was the system of apprenticeship. It was successful not only in furnishing emigrants with free transportation to America, but in profitably employing them when they reached there.

Sir George Peckham, partner in the colonization schemes of Sir Humphrey Gilbert, seems to have been the first who conceived the idea of sending out apprentices to the planta-

---
[2] Gibbins, Industry in England, p. 256.
[3] 5 Eliz. cap. 4.
[4] 43 Eliz. cap. 2.
[5] Cal. St. Pap. Col. Feb. 18, 1623.
[6] Gibbins, p. 260.

tions. In a treatise on the benefits to be derived from colonization written in 1582, he says: "There are at this day great numbers . . . which liue in such penurie & want, as could be contented to hazard their liues, and to serue one yeere for meat, drinke and apparell only, without wages, in hope thereby to amend their estates." He urges that in this way the kingdom will be greatly enlarged and strengthened, the poor relieved, and "all odious idleness from this our Realme vtterly banished."[7]

During the reign of James I. the apprenticeship system was adopted by the Virginia and London Companies as well as private adventurers. Servitude as established by these Companies differed in many respects from the indentured servitude of later years. The servant was in theory a member of the Company and served for a term of years to repay the Company for his transportation and maintenance.[8]

In order to carry out the scheme of colonization, money was raised by subscription to assist those who were willing to embark, and many who were unwilling to go were impressed as servants for the plantations. The practice of apprenticing poor children to the Virginia Company began as early as 1620. In that year, Sir Edwin Sandys petitioned Secretary Naunton for authority to send out one hundred children who had been "appointed for transportation" by the city of London, but who were unwilling to go.[9] By making use of the apprenticeship statute of Elizabeth this difficulty was removed, and both children and vagrants were regularly gathered up in London and elsewhere, and contracts made with merchants for carying them to America. To this number were added persons who were convicted of capital offences, but pardoned and transported by the order of the king.

For a number of years the involuntary emigrants prob-

---

[7] Hart's Contemporaries, I. p. 157.
[8] Ballagh, White Servitude in Virginia, p. 13.
[9] Cal. St. Pap. Col. Jan. 28, 1620.

ably outnumbered those who went of their own free wills;[10] but when the colony became firmly established, men and women willingly bound themselves to serve for a term of years in order to obtain free transportation to America.

The system of servitude thus early established in Virginia was adopted by Lord Baltimore as a means of settling and developing the colony of Maryland. Too poor to send out settlers himself, he induced others to transport servants in return for grants of land in the new colony. Many who did not wish to go in person furnished Baltimore money for transporting servants and received their pay in lands.

The servants usually signed a written contract called an indenture, which bound them to serve a master for a specified number of years in return for free transportation, food, clothing and fifty acres of land. From this contract, whether they signed it or not, all servants came to be called "indented servants."

---

[10] Hammond, Leah and Rachell, p. 7.

CHAPTER II.

THE EARLY LAND SYSTEM IN MARYLAND.

The land system in Maryland during the life of the second Lord Baltimore was very closely connected with the enterprise of importing white servants into that colony. Land was parcelled out to the adventurers directly in proportion to the number of servants brought with them from England.

Concerning the motives which led Lord Baltimore to found the colony of Maryland there has been much dispute among writers on toleration. By confining their attention to this religious controversy, they have apparently lost sight of the underlying principle in Baltimore's plans which overshadowed all others, viz., that of revenue. There is very little evidence to support the theory that Maryland was founded as a home for persecuted Catholics. A majority of the first settlers sent out were Protestants;[1] the privileges of the Catholics were limited at a very early date and their religion was not publicly allowed.[2] On the other hand, the financial difficulties of the proprietor, his instructions to his deputies, his various proclamations, and his whole scheme of colonization seem to indicate that the planting of the colony was largely a business enterprise by which Baltimore hoped to recoup his fortunes and erect for himself and his posterity a monument in the New World. When through his brother he offered land and privileges to the people of Masachusetts, he was very careful to have it understood that the new comers were to pay "such annual rent as should be agreed upon."[3]

---

[1] Johnson, Foundation of Maryland, pp. 31, 32, 73, 74; Records Eng. Prov. of Soc. of Jesus, p. 362.
[2] Rec. of Soc. of Jesus, pp. 362, 365.
[3] Winthrop's History of New England, II, 149.

Baltimore's finances in 1633 and for some time following were at a low ebb. There is a petition to the king, dated November, 1633, recorded against Baltimore and his deputy, Gabriel Hawley, setting forth "that Hawley billetted men and women for Maryland at 12d. a day in the houses of the petitioners, but took them away without giving satisfaction for their entertainment amounting to about £60, and Lord Baltimore refers them for payment to Hawley, now a prisoner in the Fleet." [4] He was dependent upon his father-in-law, Lord Arundel, for the support of himself and his family. Lord Arundel says in a letter to Windebanke, Secretary of the Treasury, "My son Baltimore is brought so low with his setting forward the plantations of Maryland and with the clamorous suits and oppositions which he hath met withal in the business as that I do not see how he could subsist if I did not give him his diet for himself, his wife, his children, and his servants." [5]

Among the inducements held out by Baltimore to secure settlers for his colony the material advantages were always put in the foreground. Rewards, station, and lands were offered in return for transporting people to Maryland.[6] Governor Stone received his appointment upon the express condition of his bringing in a specified number of colonists.[7]

Baltimore's scheme of settlement was one devised to secure as much revenue as possible from the new colony. Everything was done to settle the plantation as rapidly as possible, and as a means to this end, he resorted to the practice of importing servants on a large scale, a custom already familiar in Virginia.

Up to 1682 the distribution of land was based almost entirely upon the importation of servants. There was no such thing as direct purchase of land from the proprietor.

---

[4] Cal. State Pap. Col., Nov., 1633.
[5] Cal. State Pap. Col., Feb. 17, 1639.
[6] See account of Md. Fund. Pub., No. 7, p. 46.
[7] Scharf, History of Md. II., 12-13.

Each settler who came into the province received one hundred acres of land, but if he wished more he could obtain it only by importing servants. Sometimes large tracts of land were granted to Baltimore's personal friends without the importation of servants, but this formed a very small fraction of the land granted.

The plan upon which Maryland was founded was extremely aristocratic. It was intended to set up a landed aristocracy similar to the old manorial system. To a landless Englishman the thought of ruling over a large manor in Maryland was very attractive. He did not stop to consider the vast difference between an English manor and a barren tract in Maryland. Baltimore and his agents therefore had no difficulty in finding persons who in return for a tract of land were willing either to embark with a body of servants or to furnish them money for transporting men and women to Maryland.

The first instruments of government were instructions from the proprietor called "Conditions of Plantation." They were issued from time to time and regulated in detail the amount of land to be granted for each servant transported, and the amount of quit rent due the proprietor. The first of these conditions was issued August 8, 1636, to Leonard Calvert, governor of Maryland. The amount of land granted the adventurers varied according to the year the persons were transported. Every "first adventurer," or those who came in 1633-34, were allowed 2,000 acres of land at a yearly rent of 400 pounds of wheat for every five men servants transported. Those who transported less than five servants in the same year were allowed for each, 100 acres at a yearly rent of 20 pounds of wheat. Fifty acres were granted for bringing in children under sixteen years of age.[8] Those who brought in servants in 1634 and 1635 received but half as much land for their transportation as

---

[8] Arch. of Maryland, Vol. III., 47-48; Kilty, Land-holder's Assistant, 30-31; Bozman, Sketch of Hist. of Md., 283-285.

those who came in 1633-34, and the rent was 600 pounds of wheat per manor instead of 400 pounds. For 1635 and until further conditions should be issued the rating was fixed at 1,000 acres for every five men servants transported at an annual rent of twenty shillings to be paid in commodities of the country. If less than five servants were transported the master received for each man servant 100 acres; for maid servants and children 50 acres at a rent of twelve pence per annum.[9]

The same "Conditions" introduced into Maryland the old manorial system which continued throughout the proprietary government and traces of which may be seen even in the present day. The governor was authorized to erect every tract of 1,000 acres or more into a manor to be named in accordance with the wishes of the adventurer. Authority was also given the governor to grant to the holder of every such manor the privilege of holding a court-baron and court-leet. It is the opinion of Bozman that these courts were "probably never used," [10] but in one case at least we have existing evidence of the contrary in the manuscript records of the St. Clement's Manor preserved in the Library of the Maryland Historical Society.[11]

Besides the lands granted by the first "Conditions of Plantation," Baltimore authorized his brother to grant to the "first adventurers" ten acres of land in the town of St. Mary's for every person transported. Five acres were to be allotted to succeeding adventurers who came prior to 1638. This land was granted in free hold.[12] The second "Conditions" were promulgated in November, 1641, to take effect the following year at the feast of Annunciation. Both adventurers and servants were limited to persons of

---

[9] Arch. of Maryland, Vol. III. 47-48; Kilty, Land-holder's Assistant, 30-31; Bozman, Sketch of Hist. of Md., 283-285.
[10] Hist. of Md., p. 287.
[11] Printed in full in John Johnson's "Old Maryland Manors." J. H. Univ. Studies I. No. 7, 1883.
[12] Kilty, Land-holder's Assistant, 32-33.

"British or Irish descent." It now required that twenty able bodied men be transported in order to obtain a manor of 2,000 acres. Those who brought less than twenty servants were allowed but 50 acres for each and twenty-five acres for children under sixteen years. The quit rent was changed to forty shillings sterling per annum for each manor of 2,000 acres and twelve pence sterling per fifty acres for the small tracts, both to be paid in "commodities of the country." These smaller grants were "to be holden of some Mannor of his Lo$^{pps.}$ . . . in free socage." No claims to land were to be valid unless presented within a year after the transportation had taken place.[13]

Baltimore gives as his reasons for reducing the amount of land for each servant that the land would soon be taken up by a scattered population.[14] This would interfere with future immigration. It was to his interest to have the land more densely populated in order to develop it and enable him to increase the quit rents.

New conditions were issued in August, 1648, which were still more favorable to the proprietor but which also gave some new privileges to the adventurers and servants. The amount of land for transporting a servant remained the same; but instead of the rents being paid in commodities at the option of the planter they were to be paid in gold, silver or commodities at the option of the proprietor.

For the first time, provision was made for disposing of lands by sale. The sixth part of every manor was made demesne land which could never be alienated for a period exceeding seven years, but all the rest might be sold in fee simple to persons of Irish or British descent. This would have been a great step toward the freedom of the land holder if the land had possessed any market value, but it was counteracted to a great extent by the provision that the

---

[13] Arch. of Md., III. pp. 99-101; Kilty, 33-35.
[14] Arch. of Md. I. 331.

lands so disposed of in fee simple were subject to the same rents and services to the proprietor forever, as was required by the original grant.

In case the full number of servants were not transported and actually residing on the land, the planter forfeited to the proprietor two bushels of wheat yearly for each delinquent; and at the end of three years the proprietor was at liberty to seize upon fifty acres for each servant wanting and rent it to some one else for a term not exceeding twenty-one years, returning to the original holder a tenth part of the rent received in excess of the original quit rent.

These Conditions of 1648 were the first that made any provison for freed servants. All persons of British or Irish descent having served their full time were to be considered planters and granted the same amount of land as though they had transported themselves. All claims for land not presented within a year after due were declared invalid.[15]

Although the formal instructions limited the grants of land to persons of British or Irish descent, a commission from Baltimore to Governor Stone, enclosed at the same time, permitted him to grant lands to French, Dutch and Italian settlers in all cases where he thought it expedient.

In July, 1649, Baltimore revoked all former instructions because they "are not like to Give sufficient encouragement to many to adventure" and issued new Conditions which differ from those of 1648 only in making more liberal grants to the adventurers. The amount for importing a servant was again raised to 100 acres at a rent of two shillings sterling.[16] No expressed provision is made for freed servants, but there is every reason to believe that they continued to receive land on the expiration of their service the same as before, and by the instructions to the Lieutenant Governor, dated November 12, 1656, every servant having served his

---

[15] Arch. of Md. III. 223-228; Kilty, 38-43.
[16] Kilty, 47-51.

Early Land System in Maryland.

time and proved himself faithful to his Lordship is to receive fifty acres at an annual rent on one shilling sterling.[17] It will be seen from the above regulations that while the quit rents were never excessive the proprietor was ever mindful of his own interests and increased the rents as rapidly as the conditions would permit without discouraging immigration. From a small payment of wheat in 1636 the rent was considerably increased and rated in sterling in 1641; while in 1648, the proprietor might exact the rents in gold or silver. In September, 1658, he instructed the governor to raise the rent from one shilling to two shillings for every fifty acres.[18] Servant laborers were necessary in order to make the land more productive and capable of paying rent, and Baltimore secured the passage of laws requiring every planter who received land to keep at least three able bodied servants above sixteen years of age.[19] This created a ready market for servants and built up a lucrative trade for speculators.

We should naturally expect to find the planters eager to secure as much land as possible for their trouble and expense of bringing servants from England and at once entering claims for the fulfillment of the contract; but the contrary seems to have been the case. They had transported the servants as a means of obtaining grants of land and not because they cared especially for their labor; but when they arrived in Maryland their ideas concerning advantages to be derived from large estates seem to have undergone a sudden change. The real value of undeveloped tracts was at once apparent. Instead of demanding the lands due them they often neglected or absolutely refused to accept them. All the anxiety for an early distribution is exhibited on the part of the proprietor. The planters were not at all eager to begin paying rents on lands which were of little

---
[17] Kilty, p. 55.
[18] Kilty, pp. 55-57.
[19] Arch. of Md., Vol. I. 479, 500.

use to them and in many cases preferred to sacrifice their claims altogether. In all the conditions except the first, Baltimore warns the planters that those not presenting their claims within a year after due will lose all right to lands forever. In a proclamation of Lieutenant-Governor Stone, April 13, 1649, it is stated that many adventurers have not only neglected but *refused* to receive lands due by virtue of the several Conditions, although some of these lands have been due "by a space of divers years past." This, he says, "can produce no good effect to any adventurers . . . and his Lordship thereby also receives great prejudice in the non-payment of rents for a long time which are due and payable unto him from such adventurers or planters if they had or did take grants of all such lands due unto them in convenient time as they ought to have done." He gives those residing within the province until the following November, and those who have claims but are now residing in Virginia, until the following March, to present their claims, "and all such persons . . . who shall neglect or refuse to comply herewith must blame their own obstinancy if hereafter they be refused any such Grants." [20] Even this threat did not secure the desired effect, and the time was extended by three successive proclamations, indicating that the planters did not consider the lands with the attached quit rents very desirable possessions.

When we compare the value of the land at that time with the amount of rents we can readily understand why the planters were willing to allow their claims to lapse. The value of land in terms of other commodities is easily ascertained from the appraisement of property belonging to the estates of deceased persons. In an inventory of the property of one Robert Tutty, who died in 1647, there are three articles, each valued at 200 pounds of tobacco, viz.,

---

[20] Arch. of Md. III. 229-230; Kilty, 44-45. A similar proclamation had already been issued in 1642—Arch. III. 129.

"one yeareling Steer," "one Gun and shott bagge," and "100 acres of land due by conditions of plantation." In the same year an inventory was taken of the property of Leonard Calvert, deceased. In it a large framed house, with 100 acres of town land, is valued at 4,000 pounds of tobacco and cask; also a large house, with three manors belonging to it, is valued at 7,000 pounds of tobacco.[21]

Besides quit rents there were reliefs upon the alienation of lands. The conditions of 1648 allowed the planters the privilege of disposing of five-sixths of the lands granted them in fee simple. But on every transfer, either by sale, gift or inheritance, a relief was exacted by the lord of the manor. The amount of this relief was one whole year's income from the land exchanged.[22] The regulation and collection of reliefs was apparently one of the principal duties of the Courts Baron and Courts Leet. The following examples selected from the manuscript records of St. Clement's Manor (Oct., 1672) will suffice to show the connection of these courts with the land reliefs:

"We present that Raphaell Haywood hath aliened his ffreehold to Simon Ryder upon which alienacon there is a reliefe due to the lord," and

"We present that upon the death of Mr. Robt. Sly there is a relief due to the lord and that Mr. Gerard Sly is his next heire who hath sworn fealty accordingly." [23] It is not at all likely that the income from these reliefs was very large during the life of the first proprietor. When every immigrant and every freed servant might receive land free of charge, when, indeed, planters refused grants for services already performed, there was probably little traffic in real estate.

In 1637, a land office was created and put in charge of

---

[21] Arch. of Md. IV. 318, 321.
[22] Instructions of Baltimore, Kilty, 55-57.
[23] MS. Rec. of St. Clement's Manor; also Mayer, Ground rents in Md. App. p. 156.

John Lewger, secretary of the province.[24] As soon as it was opened, persons who had brought servants from England or Virginia presented themselves and had their respective claims recorded. They might at the same or a subsequent time demand warants of survey for a corresponding number of acres. All warrants were issued by the governor or by the secretary under his direction. Besides the demands made for importing servants, some were based on special warrants from the proprietor on such terms as had been agreed upon by himself and the individual adventurers. "The claims, being thus admitted on record," says Kilty, "stood, as it were, to the credit of the parties until they saw occasion to use or assign them."[25]

In the early land records there are two kinds of entries pertaining to servants and lands. The first are declarations of date of arrival and the number and names of all persons imported by each adventurer. The amount of land granted was determined by the number of persons brought into the province and the Conditions of Plantation in force at the time of the transportation. The following are examples of these declarations:

"Entered by Captain Evelin for the Manor of Evelinton in the Baronie of St. Marie's Thomas H., David W., Randall R., etc., to the number of 23."

"Entered by John Lewger, Secretary, brought into the province in the year 1637, John Lewger, senior, Ann his wife, John Lewger, Jun. aged 9 years, M. W., A. B. M. W., maid servants . . . and others to the number of 22."[26]

The second class of entries are the "demands." The following were selected from the many found in the land records:

"29th August 1642, Thomas Weston demandeth twelve hundred acres of land due by Conditions of Plantation for

---

[24] Kilty, p. 65.
[25] Ibid. p. 66.
[26] Ibid. p. 68.

transporting himself and 5 able men into the Province, in the year 1640, whose names are," etc.

"15th November 1642, Anthony Penruddock, Esq., assignee of Mr. Edward Robinson, Esq., by his attorney Thomas Carey demandeth 2000 acres of land due by Conditions of Plantation to the said Edward Robinson for adventuring in his Lordship's hands £100 in the first descent of the Colony for the transporting of 5 men."[27] This last demand with others of the same nature, is further evidence that Baltimore was furnished money to carry out his scheme of settlement in return for tracts of land. Unfortunately, many of the records have been destroyed, and, as we have seen above, some neglected to present their claims, otherwise we might be able to determine with certainty the number of persons imported into Maryland from the founding, in 1633-4, till the abolition of the system by Charles Calvert in 1682-3. The average number of servants for which land was granted in the early years was about six for each adventurer; some brought over as many as twenty, and some even a greater number. From 1634 to 1651, Captain Cornwallis claimed land for importing 71 servants.[28] The largest grant to any individual for bringing in immigrants which I have found in the records is a grant of 32,000 acres in Cecil county, given to Councillor George Talbott, of Castle Roovery, Roscommon county, Ireland, for transporting 640 persons within twelve years. This patent is dated June 11, 1680.[29]

When Charles Calvert succeeded his father as proprietor in 1675, the population had increased and the resources had been developed to such an extent that special inducements for transporting servants were no longer necessary. The labor of the servants now possessed an economic value, and transporting for sale had become a regular business.

---

[27] Kilty, 68-69.
[28] See this and other lists in Neill, Founders of Md.
[29] Calvert, MSS. Fol. V. No. 223.

At first, the servants usually served the masters who brought them into the colony, but after a few years regular contractors began to import them to sell to the planters and themselves receive the certificates for the lands. This enabled the contractors to secure large tracts of the best land and sell it out to the planters at an enhanced price. The old system of distribution was abolished in 1683 and a new one adopted, under which all persons might receive lands on payment of a definite amount of money, called "caution money," because no warrant could issue until it was paid or secured. Notes of hand were not accepted. All grants except for a money (i. e., tobacco) payment were strictly forbidden. The price of land was fixed at 100 pounds and 50 pounds per 50 acres, according to location, both at the annual rent of 4 shillings per 100 acres.[30] In 1712, a money rent was substituted for that of tobacco.[31] Baltimore, in a certificate sent to the British government, justifies his abolition of old Conditions of Plantation on the ground that the colonial official took advantage of the planters by buying up the claims of the merchants and ship officers and selling them to the planters at an enhanced price, which was a great injustice to the poorer classes.

"My father used to allow fifty acres of land for every servant imported, as to which the transporter had to take oath that he never had the benefits of the conditions of plantation, termed, rights to land in Maryland. These rights have of late years been mostly bought up from merchants and commanders by the Collectors and Deputy Surveyors of the province, who often disposed of the same to the poorer inhabitants at excessive rates. I therefore thought good to alter these conditions of plantation, and instead of a right due upon the transportation of a servant, for which the Collector often charged four hundred weight of tobacco, I declared that I would accept one hundred

---

[30] Kilty, 121, 122.
[31] Ibid. 128.

weight of tobacco for every fifty acres, with which all classes of the inhabitants are much better satisfied." [32]

Baltimore might have added another reason for the change, that it increased his income, now dependent solely upon the quit rents and alienation dues, by adding to it the original purchase money from all new lands yet to be taken up in the province.

The amount of income to the proprietor from quit rents during the seventeenth and the first half of the eighteenth centuries cannot be determined with any degree of certainty, but from a report made to the legislature in 1745 the amount given is £4568, 15s, 4d, and "from the best estimates which can be collected from the debt books, it appears that, in the year 1770, their gross amount was about £8400 sterling, and the net revenue of the proprietor from them, after deducting the expenses of collection, upwards of £7500." [33]

We have confined our attention thus far to the lands received by the adventurers for transporting servants and others in Maryland; let us now consider the lands received by the servants when their term of servitude had expired. Until 1648, no provision was made by the proprietor for granting lands to freed servants, but the conditions of plantation for that year allowed them as many acres as those who had transported themselves, provided they were of British or Irish descent. This, of course, was to be taken from the lands of the proprietor. Some time before this, however, provision had been made for freed servants by the provincial legislature. By an act of the General Assembly, October 23, 1640, one of the items enumerated in the freedom due is "ffifty acres of land five whereof at least to be plantable." [34] This law continued in force until 1663. The five-acres clause was considered a great burden by the planters, as it

---

[32] Cal. State Pap. Col. May, 1683.
[33] McMahon, Hist. Views, 171-172.
[34] Arch. of Md. I. 97.

canceled in a great measure the profits derived from the labor of the servants, which could not have been very large in the early years of the colony. The repealing act was passed in the September term, 1663, and the reason given is the *incapacity* of the inhabitants to fulfill the conditions. An *ex post facto* clause was added, which excluded servants freed before the repeal from all benefit of the former act.[35] The freed servant could no longer require land from his former master unless it was expressly stipulated in the indenture, which was sometimes the case, as may be seen in the court procedings. The repeal of the law of 1640 did not affect the condition of the freedman materially until 1683, when the conditions of plantations were abolished by the proprietor, for he could always obtain free land by applying to the governor.

It does not appear from the court proceedings that the servant always received land as a part of the freedom dues from the master, or that he always demanded it, even while the law of 1640 was in force. In a suit brought by Henry Spink, in 1648, against Cuthbert Fenwick, administrator of the estate of Nicholas Harvey, the court was called upon to define the "custom of the country," and "The court fowned one cap or hatt, one cloak or frize suite, one shirt one pr shoes & stockins one axe one broad and one narrow hoe, 50 acres of Land, and 3 barrells Corne."[36] This case is interesting from another point of view. Besides the freedom dues, the servant claimed a certain amount of tobacco which was owed him by his deceased master. Fenwick had refused to pay either the freedom dues or the other debt, on the ground that an administrator could not be compelled to pay the debts of an estate within a year and a day after the decease of the owner. But the court ruled that "the privilege of an administ^r was not to be extended to the case of serv^{ts} wages." The defendant was ordered to pay the

---

[35] Arch. of Md. I. 496.
[36] Arch. of Md. IV. 361.

servant whatever was due by custom of the country as already defined by the judge, but the payment of the other debt was postponed as coming under the privilege of the administrator. In other words his claims as a *freedman* were allowed while his claims as a *freeman* were denied.

Other cases in the court records might be cited in which land is included in the custom of the country. On the other hand, in some of the suits for freedom dues during the same period land is mentioned neither in the petition of the servant nor in the order of court. For example, one Robert Jones, servant of John Nunn, in 1653, sued in court for clothes, etc., according to the custom of the country. He was allowed clothes, ax, hoe, etc., and damages for attending court several times, but no land is mentioned.[37] Likewise, in the following year, the court ruled that "Whereas Joseph Edwards hath Served out his time of Service due by Indenture to Mr. Arthur Turner. . . . It is ordered that the Said Turner Shall pay . . . the Said Edwards three Barrells of Corne," etc.; but here again is no mention of land.[38] The omission of land in the last instance might be due to the fact that Edwards was a servant by indenture and land may not have been stipulated in the contract, but in the case of Jones above mentioned and others found in the court records they were servants by custom of the country, and by law entitled to fifty acres of land.

Still another phase of the question is illustrated by the case of a servant, John Norman, against his master, Edward Bowles, May, 1654, in which land was allowed by the court, but the corn, clothes, etc., were refused, because they were not included in the indenture.[39] It is hard to determine from these various interpretations of the custom of the country whether the law requiring a grant of land as a part of the freedom dues was regularly carried out or not.

[37] Arch. of Md. X. 161, 325.
[38] Arch. X. 406.
[39] Arch. X. 382.

We have, however, found no case in the records where land was demanded by the servant that the court did not allow the claim.

With the abolition of the Conditions of Plantation by Charles Calvert in 1683, all connection between the distribution of land and the importation of servants came to an end. The latter now became purely an item of traffic between the importer and the planter who stood in need of the labor of the servant.

CHAPTER III.

NUMBER AND ECONOMIC IMPORTANCE.

The actual number of servants imported into Maryland and the ratio which they bore to the free inhabitants cannot easily be determined from the scanty records which have been left us. All historians of Maryland complain of the dearth of contemporaneous material. Outside of the purely legal documents, the settlers have left us very few journals or records of historical value. If the provisions of the laws were carried out, there are many valuable statistics which must have been collected, but which have not been found. For example, the laws required that all servants who entered the province should be registered at the county courts. One member of the Assembly of 1663 was enterprising enough to raise the question whether it would not be wise for the Secretary to preserve a list of all servants and passengers transported into Maryland. He was voted down by a vote of five to one, the Chancellor deciding that it was unnecessary.[1] No custom house record of passengers has been found earlier than the latter part of the nineteenth century. A law was passed by the Congress of the United States, in 1819, requiring an exact list of all immigrants entering the various ports of the United States to be sent to the State Department. This was done at first, but apparently only one such report was ever made. What few records are available concerning the number of servant immigrants come mainly from British sources.

There were no great migrations of peoples from Europe to Maryland which attracted the attention of travelers and writers, as did the arrival of the Palatines in New York and

---

[1] Arch. of Md. I. 469.

Pennsylvania. The growth of population in Maryland was more gradual. All foreigners were welcomed, and none became dominant. The large number of Germans in New York and Pennsylvania attracted many of their countrymen to visit them and write about them, while travelers who visited Baltimore and Annapolis usually confined their remarks to the soil, the climate, and the negroes.

For some time after the founding of the colony, the servants came exclusively from Great Britain, Ireland, and Virginia. Of the original immigrants the ratio of servants to freeman was probably about 6 to 1.[2]

In the Assembly of 1637, which all freemen were required to attend, only 90 appeared either in person or by proxy, leaving about 220 who must have been servants. This would make the ratio at this time 7 to 3. The increase in the proportion of freemen was due to the expiration of some of the servants' terms and to the immigration from Virginia.

Among the Calvert Papers is a manuscripe which gives some clue to the proportion of servants a few years later. It is marked, "A note of all Warrants for the Granting of Land in Maryland." The document is undated, but the last entry is dated January 23, 1658, so the report was probably made out and sent to Baltimore about that time. It gives the names of the adventurers, the amount of land granted them, and the number of servants they had transported or were to transport within the next four years. The number of immigrants for whom land is received is 1078. This number does not represent the actual number of servants in Maryland at that time, as none of them were to be transported in future. On the other hand, we have seen that some neglected to claim land for the servants whom they had brought in with them. The number thus omitted in the report is probably as large or larger than

---

[2] Johnson, Foundation of Maryland, 173.

the number to be transported in future, therefore the number given in the report is doubtless very nearly the number in the province. The number of inhabitants in Maryland in 1660 is given by Kennedy as 12,000.[3] A comparison of the two numbers gives the ratio of servants to freemen at about 1 to 11. This great increase of freemen over servants was due to the large influx from Virginia. By far the larger number of settlers for the first thirty years came from that colony. The Virginians complained that one-half of their province was depopulated to settle Maryland.[4] Most of the European immigrants at this time came from Great Britain and Ireland; later, the number was increased by arrivals from France, Holland, Bohemia, Spain, and Italy. Before 1649 there was very little inducement offered to foreigners except English and Irish. They were allowed neither land nor political rights. In that year the proprietor issued a proclamation allowing his brother to grant land to all foreigners, but they were not accorded full protection of the laws of the province until 1674.[5] With the exception of the Dutch, Swiss, and Germans, who came in large numbers in later years, very few of the immigrants from the continent came over as servants. In the notice of runaways given in the newspapers we occasionally come across a Frenchman, Swede, or even Jew, but the number is very small.

The census of Maryland taken in 1752 gives the number of free inhabitants as 98,357 servants, 6,870; convicts, 1,981.[6] This, again, gives the ratio of servants and convicts to the free population at about 1 to 11. From this, it would seem that the proportion of servants remained practically constant, and if so it would mean that quite a large proportion of the freemen had at one time been servants.

---

[3] Hist. and Statistics of Md. p. 19.
[4] Allen, Who were the Early Settlers of Maryland, p. 4.
[5] Arch. of Md. II. 400-401.
[6] Griffith, Early Hist. of Md. p. 54.

Virginia, Pennsylvania, and Maryland were the three great servant-importing colonies. One of Maryland's historians asserts that there were more servants there than in any other colony.[7] There is no authority given for this statement, and it is probably an exaggeration. She doubtless did possess as many to the square mile as any other colony, but in Pennsylvania, whose area is much greater, and where the German immigration was very large, there must have been a greater number of servants than in Maryland. Governor Sharpe, in a letter to Lord Baltimore in 1756, states that there are at that time more servants in Maryland and Pennsylvania than in all the other colonies together. "The people," he says, "cannot well manage their Business without their Assistance."[8] This, coming from a contemporary and one who had investigated the matter in order to ascertain the number that were available for military service, may be accepted as true.

The newspapers record the arrival of large numbers of servants and convicts at the ports of Baltimore and Annapolis, but these records are fragmentary and incomplete. Hardly a ship arrived that did not bring from twenty to fifty and sometimes one hundred indentured servants or convicts.

At first the religious liberty in Maryland drew large numbers of Irish to that province. They became so numerous that the Protestants became alarmed and imposed heavy duties on Irish servants, in order to prohibit their importation. Besides the religious prejudice which they naturally entertained against the Catholics, the Protestants feared that they would assist the French in the struggle of the two nations for the possession of America.[9] The first duty on servants was imposed by the act of 1696. This was fol-

---

[7] Brantly, The English in Maryland, p. 29; also Winsor's Nar. and Crit. Hist. III. 545.
[8] Arch. of Md. VI. p. 477.
[9] Doyle, Eng. Cols. in Am. 316, 317.

lowed by several acts laying duty on Irish Catholic servants.[10] The law of 1704 fixed the duty on Irish Catholics at twenty shillings per poll, while all Protestant servants came in free. In 1717, the duty was raised to forty shillings and a fine of £500 was imposed upon all who evaded paying the duty. The last act of the kind was passed in 1773, and was to continue in force for twenty-one years.[11]

These laws greatly lessened the number of Irish servants sent to Maryland, but, as Scharf remarks, some, "like the wheat-fly, showed themselves in spite of precaution."[12] Governor Sharpe speaks of their presence in 1756, and says that they are "excluded" from military duty.[13] As they were also banished from Virginia,[14] the greater number of Irish Catholics were sent to Jamaica and other islands.[15]

In the latter half of the eighteenth century the number of servants was increased by the arrival of large numbers of Dutch, Swiss, and Germans. Schultz[16] says that the first known German settlers in Maryland were those among the Dutch and French Labadists, who located on Bohemian Manor in 1681; but there is evidence of their presence as early as 1674, for among the foreigners who petitioned for political privileges in 1674 are French, Swedes, Danes, Germans, and Dutch.[17] They did not, however, come in very large numbers till some time later, and there is no evidence that any of them became servants at this early date.

No considerable number of Germans seem to have come to Maryland till about the middle of the eighteenth century, and as they came, at first, largely from Pennsylvania, they were doubtless nearly all free inhabitants. Fredericktown

---

[10] Bacon's Laws 1699 Ch. XXIII.; 1704, Ch. XXXIII.; 1708, Ch. XVI.; 1715, Ch. XLIX.; 1719, Ch. XVI.
[11] Green's Laws of Md. June, 1773, Ch. 2.
[12] Hist. of Md. I. 370-371.
[13] Letter to Lords of Trade, Arch. VI. 353.
[14] Narrative of Father White, Fund Pub. No. 7, p. 29.
[15] Cal. State Pap. various items.
[16] First Settlements of Germans in Md. p. 4.
[17] Arch. of Md. II. 400, 401.

was settled in 1732 by Pennsylvanians and became the nucleus of the large German settlements in western Maryland. There is no record of Palatine immigrants having come to Maryland before the arrival of the ship Integrity, in September, 1752, but the entries at Annapolis show that 1060 came between 1752 and 1755.[18] It is estimated that the whole number of Germans who came to Maryland between 1748 and 1754 is about 2800.[19] Many of these settled in Baltimore, and, in 1754, formed nearly the entire population of that city.[20] They continued in rapidly increasing numbers till long after the Revolution.

The records are not sufficiently complete for us to ascertain with any degree of accuracy the proportion of servants and redemptioners among the German immigrants, but the newspaper records of their arrival, the accounts given by writers (such as Eddis, Fearon, Mittleberger, and Muhlenberg) who describe the restitution and harsh treatment of a large number of German immigrants, and the fact that societies were formed and laws enacted for the sole purpose of protecting poor Germans who were unable to discharge the debt for the passage, all indicate that a large number of these immigrants were obliged to serve for a term of years. Another indication that a large proportion of the German and Dutch immigrants to Maryland belonged to that class who were unable to "pay their freight" is the remarkable falling off in the whole number of German immigrants after laws were passed which made it unprofitable to deal in servants.

The economic importance of the servant in developing the resources of the colonies, especially in the middle colonies, can hardly be overestimated. All the provinces were essentially agricultural, but the large tobacco plantations of

---

[18] Fifth Annual Report of the German Soc. of Md. Records of subsequent arrivals are missing.

[19] Rupp's Collection of 3,000 Names of Immigrants in Penn. p. 12.

[20] Letter of Sharpe to Lord Baltimore, May 2, 1754. Arch. of Md. VI. p. 57.

Maryland and Virginia made a large supply of cheap laborers more necessary there than in the northern colonies. Maryland's geographical position made her especially dependent upon the labor of servants and convicts. She formed the border line between the plantation system of the South and the diversified industry of the North, and possessed, therefore, many of the characteristics of both. Her soil and climate were especially adapted for large tobacco plantations, which created a great demand for laborers; but, while Virginia and the other southern provinces depended very largely upon slave labor at an early date, it was many years before slaves in Maryland took the place of white servants. The combination of the plantation system of the South with the white labor system of the North made servant labor in Maryland a very important factor. Maryland early became one of the leading tobacco-growing colonies, and continued to hold her place in the first rank throughout the colonial period. Postelthwayte,[21] writing in 1774, says that Maryland produced "as much, or more, in quantity than Virginia." The Labadists, Dankers and Sluyter, who traveled in Maryland in 1679, speak of the fertility of the soil and the large quantities of tobacco produced there. So rich was the soil that the planters have been raising tobacco on the same ground thirty years. "So large a quantity of tobacco," say the travelers, "is raised in Maryland and Virginia that it is one of the greatest sources of revenue to the crown by reason of the taxes which it yields.[22] In the culture of tobacco a large number of servants, as well as some slaves, were employed. They produced on an average about 2500 to 3000 pounds of tobacco annually.

No system of free labor could have been maintained in the plantation colonies until a comparatively late date. In the

---

[21] Dictionary of Commerce, Vol. I.
[22] Journal of a Voyage to New York in Memoirs of the Long Island Hist. Soc. I. p. 216.

first place, the poor of Europe would not have been able to come to America, had they been obliged to pay for their passage in advance. On the other hand, the planters could not afford to pay the wages of free laborers. Even with the large supply of servants and convicts, free labor was high and unprofitable. Laborers would not hire, except for very high wages, when they could easily obtain new lands and become planters themselves. Winthrop records an instance of the seventeenth century which illustrates the conditions in a colony which depended very largely on free labor.

"I may upon this occasion report a passage between one of Rowley and his servant. The master, being forced to sell a pair of his oxen to pay his servant his wages, told his servant he could keep him no longer, not knowing how to pay him next year. The servant answered him, he would serve him for more of his cattle. But how shall I do (saith the master) when all my cattle are gone? The servant replied, you shall then serve me, and so you may have your cattle again." [23] It was the scarcity of laborers that made the sale of convicts easy, in spite of the sentiment against them.

The great importance of the servant's labor is shown during the French and Indian war by the attitude of the planters toward enlistment. They were willing to expose the colony to invasion and to defy the authority of their own and the British government rather than allow their servants to join the army. Even Governor Sharpe, himself an army officer and one who was doing all in his power to raise recruits, admitted that the enlisting of servants would "distress the country infinitely more than a Decimation of its free Inhabitants." [24] In another letter, written to his brother John, in 1755, he speaks of the suffering caused by the loss of servants. "Many of the People's cases really called for

---

[23] Winthrop, Hist. of New Eng. II. 219, 220.
[24] Sharpe to Calvert, Arch. V. p. 483.

Pity and Redress as the Planters' Fortunes here consist in the number of their Servants (who are purchased at high Rates) much as the Estates of an English Farmer do in the Multitude of Cattle."[25]

As slavery increased in Maryland, servant labor became less indispensable, but as long as they continued to come they were preferred to slaves and always found a ready market. They were valued not only for their own labor, but as directors and overseers of the slaves. For many years the only skilled laborers in the province came as servants from England and Ireland. Manufacturing was not carried on to any great extent in Maryland till after the Revolution, but what few manufacturers there were, were servants.[26] Not only was this class of immigrants of great importance while actually serving, but when free many of them became prosperous citizens and assisted materially in developing the resources of the colony. Had it not been for the institution of servitude, many a prosperous planter and tradesman would have been forced to remain in Europe and eke out a miserable existence. Without this method of transportation, the number of immigrants would have been small indeed, and the development of the colony retarded. It is true that many who came from England and Ireland were worthless and indolent, but from their ranks came artisans and tradesmen very essential to the prosperity of a new colony. But the Germans were of greater value in developing the agricultural resources of the colony than the immigrants from any other nation. They came to make homes for themselves, and those who were obliged to serve for their own transportation made excellent servants, and when freed from their indenture they immediately set to work to develop new lands and became peaceable and prosperous citizens. German and Dutch immigrants, both freemen and servants, were appreciated by the Maryland gov-

---

[25] Arch. of Md. VI. 211.
[26] Sharpe to Bd. of Trade, Dec. 9, 1766, Arch. XIV. 359.

ernment and offered special inducements to settle there. Lord Baltimore, in 1750, issued a proclamation offering German settlers land free from rent for three years. They were to pay nothing for the land till the end of five years, and then not more than £5 for every hundred acres.[27] Again, in 1754, when a duty was imposed on other servants brought into the colony, all German, Dutch, and Flemish servants were admitted free.[28]

[27] MS. No. 3, Proprietary Papers 1708-1762.
[28] Bacon's Laws 1754, Ch. IX.

CHAPTER IV.

Indenture and "Custom of the Country."

Persons transported into the colonies and bound to serve for a term of years are usually designated by the general term of "indented servants." Strictly speaking, however, not all, and perhaps not a majority of the servants in Maryland were indentured servants.

Bound servants admit of two classifications: one based on the terms of transportation, the other on their status under the laws of the colony.

With respect to the terms of transportation, there were three classes, namely, convicts, who were sentenced to transportation by the British courts; indentured servants who signed a contract in Europe; and the so-called free-willers or redemptioners who signed no indenture in Europe, but were given a certain number of days after arriving in America in which to dispose of their labor and pay for their passage.

Under the second classification there were four types of servants recognized by the laws of Maryland and for each of which special provisions were made in nearly all the acts of assembly. These were the convicts, the servants by indenture, the hired servants, and the servants "by custom of the country."

As most servants fall under both classifications no attempt will be made to treat them in the order above given. It is necessary to keep in mind the distinction between servants by indenture and servants by custom of the country, as their social and legal status differed materially in many respects. An indentured servant was one who served under a written agreement or contract called an indenture. This contract was usually though not always drawn up and signed in the mother country just before the voyage was undertaken. Whether made in Europe or America the indenture bound the servant to the master or his assigns, stipulating definitely how long the servant was to serve and whether at some particular employment or at general labor at the option of the master. The master on his part agreed to provide the servant with food, clothing and other necessaries of life during the term of servitude. There was generally also an agreement on the part of the master to provide the servant on the expiration of his term with a specified outfit of clothing, tools, and corn. Sometimes the things to be given the servant were not enumerated but summed up in the general term of "customary freedom dues."

Whether it was customary for each party to the contract to receive a copy of it cannot be satisfactorily determined from the records. Instances are met with where the master alone possesses the indenture. In other cases, mention is made of the servant's losing his indenture or leaving it in England.

The indenture was usually entered into voluntarily by the servant and the term varied in length from one to five years, or longer in case of minors. The form of these contracts varied little, and generally in the latter part of the period printed blanks were used with the names and conditions filled in to suit the occasion.

In most cases, the reason which induced the servant to enter into such a contract was to secure passage to the plantations. In the seventeenth and eighteenth centuries very few of the poorer classes in Europe could afford to defray the expenses of a long sea voyage. Many persons, therefore, either to better their social and economic condition, to secure freedom of worship, or to escape from the officers of the law in the mother country, were willing to thus sign away their liberty for a term of years in order to obtain a free passage to the New World.

In the early part of the colonial period it was customary for a man of means when coming to America to bring with him a number of servants. In this case, where there was an indenture at all, it was made directly by master and servant. In later years, when the importation of servants came to be carried on almost entirely by merchants and ship-masters, the servant contracted with the latter with the understanding that he would be sold to some planter on arriving in America. The indenture was, therefore, made out in favor of the ship-master or his assigns, and the servant might be sold any number of times during his term of indenture.

Such indentures as before stated were usually for four or five years and were governed to a great extent by the custom of the country in the colony where the servant was to be taken. The time, however, might vary with the desire of the servant to embark. Whatever term was fixed by the indenture, whether short or long, was enforced by the laws of Maryland.

Free-willers usually signed no indenture, but when they did, the term was necessarily the same as that of the "custom" servants. If they were without money and indebted for their passage they were not in a position to demand any shorter term than was provided by law for servants without indentures. On the other hand, they could not be forced to sign for a longer term, for, by refusing to sign any indenture whatever, they could be compelled to serve only four or five years according to the "custom" at the time they were transported. In exceptional cases, they were required to serve long enough only to pay the expenses of the voyage. In an indenture made in 1803 in Baltimore a certain Adam Hoy contracts to serve Charles L. Boehme for two years, eleven months and twenty days in "Consideration of the Sum of Eighty Dollars and sixty-four cents . . . paid by Charles L. Boehme to James Brays for (my) his passage from Amsterdam to the City of Baltimore."[1] This is of

---

[1] MS. in Md. Hist. Soc. Library, Fol. 12, Letter No. 8.

interest as showing the cost of the voyage at this time. It is a sum which few poor Europeans could afford to pay, but was considerably less than the amount charged during the two preceding centuries. When servants were scarce indentures were sometimes made for as short a term as one year without any diminution of the freedom dues.

Very often indentures were made which had no connection whatever with passage money, but were entered into by servants who were already residents of Maryland. In such contracts, the regular freedom dues were sometimes the only consideration promised the servant; in other cases, the master agreed to give him an additional reward of tobacco or other commodities at the expiration of his term of servitude. Those resident servants were usually those who had served before and as they were not indebted to the master they could nearly always secure better terms.

There was another class of servants in Maryland who served by indenture and whose condition in many respects differed little from that of the immigrants who were sold to pay for their passage. These were the indentured hired servants. The principal difference was that they were better paid for their labor. They were subject to the same legal restrictions as the ordinary servant. Without the consent of their masters they were not permitted to leave their homes or to dispose of any property. Their indentures were negotiable and could be disposed of without their consent. A typical contract will illustrate how closely their position approached that of the ordinary indentured servant and how widely they differed from the hired servant of the present day. For a consideration of 6,000 pounds of tobacco already received Walter Guest on December 14, 1645, bound himself to serve Edward Fisher for a term of three years at whatever employment Fisher should choose to engage him in. The servant was bound not to absent himself at any time without the consent of his master. Beside the tobacco, the master bound himself to provide the servant with "sufficient meate lodgeing washing and apparrell" while he continued in his service. This indenture was not, as in most cases of servant hire, made out to the master, or his assigns, nevertheless it was signed over to one Thomas Moore two months later.[2] Nearly all laws inflicting penalties upon servants for running away or other misdemeanors include hired servants in the same category with the others. In most cases, they were already residents of the province and quite often former servants.

It was sometimes possible for the servant to commute the service stipulated in his indenture by making some other arrangement satisfactory to his master. The following agreement made in 1642 illustrates both indenture for a particular employment and commutation of service. A glover named Thomas Todd was indentured to John Lewger, secretary of the province of Maryland. By a written agreement he was released from his indenture on condition that he would annually prepare a certain number of skins and make them into breeches and gloves for his master.[3]

Indentures for some particular service were common. Tradesmen, clerks, and even school-masters and ministers were disposed of in this manner. "Not a ship arrives," says Boucher, "either with redemptioners or convicts in which school-masters are not as regularly advertised for sale, as weavers, tailors, or any other trade; with little other difference, that I can hear of, excepting perhaps that the former do not usually fetch so good a price as the latter." [4]

Some indentures were made conditional. In April, 1647, a certain Hannah Mathews bound herself to serve Thomas Greene of St. Mary's for four years in return for "meate drinke lodging cloathing . . . fifty akers of Land, & one yeares provision." Annexed to the indenture was an agreement stipulating that if Hannah should at any time during

---

[2] Arch. of Md. IV. pp. 327-328.
[3] Ibid. p. 283.
[4] Boucher, A View of the Causes and Consequences of the American Revolution, pp. 183-184.

the term pay to the master one thousand pounds of tobacco and three barrels of good corn "the s^d Indenture shall bee voyd, & to noe effect, & the s^d Hannah acquitted from all obligacon of service." Hannah also bound herself neither to marry nor "depart the country" until the indenture had been canceled.[5]

Analogous to the indenture was a contract sometimes given by a free person in which a promise of personal service is given as security for debt. If the debtor failed to met the obligation he had to serve till the debt was discharged.[6]

As nearly all indentures were negotiable they were regularly disposed of at auction or private sale. The following is an example of the notices which appeared in the papers whenever a servant ship arrived in port:

JUST ARRIVED
In the ship Sophia, Alexander Verdeen, Master, from
Dublin, Twenty stout, healthy Indented
MEN SERVANTS
Whose Indentures will be disposed of on reasonable
Terms, by the Captain on board, or the subscribers . . ." etc.[7]

The price received for servants varied according to their skill, age and other personal qualities, but the average price for adults seems to have been about £15 to £20.[8] Governor Sharpe in a letter to Baltimore in 1755 states that convicts were regularly sold by the contractors at £8 to £20 each.[9]

Besides the ordinary indentured servants there were many apprentices in Maryland throughout the colonial period. These were minors and were bound out by their

---

[5] Arch. of Md. IV. p. 464.
[6] Ibid. p. 482.
[7] Md. Gaz. or Balt. Adv. Dec. 27, 1785.
[8] Men-servants in Jamaica in 1670 sold for £12 to £15, women £10 to £12. Cal. St. Pap. Col. Sept. 28, 1670.
[9] Arch. of Md. VI. p. 295.

parents, guardians, or by courts. They were subject to many of the same restrictions as other servants, but also enjoyed many privileges peculiar to apprentices. No minor could be apprenticed without his own consent and the consent of his parents if they were living. Unless he signified his consent and signed the indenture in the presence of an officer the contract was void. The duties required of them were usually lighter than those of other servants and an education was generally one of the terms of the contract. Indentures of apprentices are found among the earliest records. For example, in 1648, a certain Mary Harris was indentured by her parents to Thomas Copley of St. Inegos, Maryland. In consideration of a "good Education and well bringing up" the girl was bound to serve her master for a term of ten years. The master bound himself not to dispose of the apprentice to any one whatsoever.[10] Very few, if any, of these indentures were made negotiable. Poor children were bound out by the courts long after servitude as a system had ceased to exist.

The servants who gave the most trouble to their masters and the most business to the courts and lawyers were those who were known as servants by "custom of the country." They comprised nearly all of the kidnapped servants and free-willers. Whenever convicts were successful in concealing the identity they also were included in this class.

All persons who were captured in Europe by kidnappers and sent to America were sold by the captain to the highest bidder without indenture. Free-willers by an agreement with the captain were promised a certain number of days in which to hire themselves to planters or tradesmen, but in practice they were usually sold without indenture as soon as the ship arrived in port. They were led by the captain to believe that the planters would readily advance the cost of the voyage and that they could repay him in a short time

---

[10] Arch. of Md. X. pp. 305-306.

and go free. "But scarce had they yielded to the pleasing reflection," says Eddis, "that every danger, every difficulty is happily surmounted before their fond hopes are cruelly blasted, and they find themselves involved in all the complicated miseries of a tedious, laborious, and unprofitable servitude." [11]

Where the servants were ignorant, which was usually the case, it was to the advantage of the master that there should be no written contract, as there was then a chance of extending the term of service. It was necessary, therefore, for the Assembly to make laws from time to time to protect the servant from such extension and at the same time to secure masters from unjust claims of the servant.

The Assembly of 1638-9, the first of which we have any record, passed a law "limiting the times of Servants." All indentures made by servant and master, whatever the terms might be, were to be enforced by the courts. For cases where there was no indenture the law fixed the term of service and the amount of freedom dues. All males, eighteen years of age or over—slaves excepted—who without indenture were brought into the province at the charge of another, were to serve the latter for a term of four years from their first arrival. If under eighteen years they must serve till they arrived at the age of twenty-four. The term of maid servants over twelve years of age was fixed at four years; if under twelve, seven years of service were required. On the expiration of the term thus fixed by law the master must provide every man servant with "one new Cloth sute one new Shirt one pair of new Shews one pair of new stockins and a new monmoth Capp." Each maid servant was to receive as freedom dues "one new petty coat and wast coat one new smock one pair of new Shoes one pair of new stockings and the Clothes formerly belonging to the Servant." Both men and maid servants, in addition to the

---

[11] Letters from America, pp. 72-73.

above, must be equipped with "three barrels of Corne a hilling hoe and a weeding hoe and a felling axe."[12] This act was not approved by the higher authorities, but indicates the customs of the times.

Disputes concerning the ages of servants and the length of their terms of servitude led to the passage of a law in October, 1654, which required masters to bring all servants, whether indentured or not, before the court to have their indentures recorded or their ages adjudged and registered. This must be done in the presence of the servant in order to prevent any misrepresentation on the part of the master. The servant was further protected by compelling the assigns to pay all freedom dues fixed by the court or promised by the original owner of the servant.[13] But this law proved ineffectual because no penalty was attached for neglecting to produce the servant in court. A new law was enacted in April, 1661-2, which required the master to present all servants in court for registry within three months after they came into his possession. A neglect or refusal to comply with the law deducted one year from the servant's term of bondage. All indentures or agreements made by any servant during his term of service were declared utterly void and should in no case extend the term of service.[14] In the following year (April, 1662,) an additional penalty of 1,000 pounds of tobacco was imposed for neglecting to have the servants registered in court.[15]

These regulations in favor of the servant in the early years of the colony were due, no doubt, to the presence of freedmen in the Assembly. The time lost in carrying the servants to court and the expense of having them registered was a great inconvenience to the planters. So many complaints were entered that the Assembly modified the law

---

[12] Arch. of Md. I. p. 80.
[13] Ibid. p. 352.
[14] Ibid. pp. 409-410.
[15] Ibid. p. 453.

by limiting it to servants under twenty-two years of age.[16] These minor servants were regularly carried to the courts for registration, but very few of the records have been preserved. The following is an example, taken from the Kent county records for April 20, 1676-7: "Mr. Joseph Wickes brought a woman servant to court yt came in without Indentures, named Christian Gordon who doth declare in open court yt she is nineteen years old. This court doth order yt ye s^d servant doe serve according to the Act of Assembly wch is six years from her first Arrivall."[17]

As tobacco growing became more profitable, the labor of the servant rather than land received for his transportation was the thing most valued by the planter. The term for "custom" servants was raised to five years in 1666, as it was claimed that in four years the master could not "receive that reasonable satisfaction for the charges, trouble & greate hazard" of importing and maintaining them.[18] The real cause for the change, however, was the increased importance of servants' labor rather than the reason given by the Assembly.

Although the Assembly yielded to the demands of the planters and lengthened the term of servitude, nevertheless they continued to protect the servant in whatever privileges were allowed him and to shield him from frauds very often attempted by the master. The lower house drew up a bill in 1674 which provided that unless the indenture was produced in court within six months after the servant's arrival in the provinces the term should be fixed by the court. This term was to stand, regardless of any indenture which might subsequently be produced by either party. The upper house refused to assent to the bill unless some exception should be made in favor of servants who had accidentally left their indenture in England, or in cases "where by

---

[16] Arch. of Md. I. pp. 443-444.
[17] Hanson, Old Kent of Md. p. 298.
[18] Arch. of Md. II. 147.

undue means the Master should get the Serv^{ts} Indenture out of his hands and thereby debarre him of the Priviledge of Shewing the same to the C^{rt} to the greate wrong & Injurie of the Servt."[19]

Freemen might for certain offences be sentenced by the courts to serve for a term of years. By a law of 1654, anyone who stole goods from an inhabitant of the province could be compelled either to restore four times their value or to make satisfaction by servitude.[20] In all such cases no indenture was made out, the entry in the court records being sufficient.

So many obnoxious conditions had crept into the indentures which the German redemptioners were induced to sign that in 1817 a complete change was made in the laws relating both to indentured and "custom" servants. Adults, whether indentured or not, could be held to serve only four years. Minors were set free at twenty-one and eighteen years of age, according to sex, no matter what agreement had been previously made. No agreement made in Europe or elsewhere bound a servant to serve for the passage of another, dead or alive.[21] From this on there was practically no distinction between indentured servants and those by custom of the country.

---

[19] Arch. of Md. II. pp. 351, 352.
[20] Ibid. I. p. 344.
[21] Laws of Md. Dec. Sess. 1817.

CHAPTER V.

Fugitive Servants.

One of the most noticeable features of indentured servitude, and one which greatly impeded the successful operation of the institution, was the large number of runaways. From the founding of the colony to the dying out of white servitude in the first half of the nineteenth century there is abundant evidence that large numbers of servants deserted the service of their masters, and their apprehension was one of the most serious problems with which the planters had to deal.

When we consider the class of persons who made up the servant body and the conditions under which they very often entered into servitude, we need not be surprised at the great number of fugitives, but, on the contrary, we find ourselves wondering why there were not more. This desertion from service was due to several causes, and the blame attaches sometimes to the servant, sometimes to the master or the speculator, and very often to neither, but to the inherent evils of the institution itself. Often the servant when captured gave as his reasons for running away that his master did not provide sufficient food and clothing or had treated him cruelly. Investigation sometimes proved this to be the case; at other times, it was found to be only an excuse.

Another class of servants ran away as soon as they discovered the deception that had been practiced upon them by the contractors who had induced them to come to America. They had been led to believe by accounts published in such tracts as Alsop's Character of the Province of Maryland and from the stories of wealth, ease, and luxury told them by agents whose business it was to drum up recruits for transportation that the life of a servant was an easy one, and that it was a stepping-stone to fame and fortune. These "agents or crimps," writes Eddis, who had often seen their advertisements in London, "represent the advantages to be obtained in America, in colors so alluring that it is almost impossible to resist their artifices."[1] Many of these immigrants had no intention of binding themselves to servitude, but were led by the agents to believe that laborers were so eagerly sought after and wages so high that they might by hiring for a short time to some planter pay back the passage money and go free. Disappointed in their expectations and forced by necessity into a distasteful bondage, their only thought was to escape by running away from their master, even though he may have treated them kindly. Eddis gives an interesting account of a young man who was purchased by a Maryland gentleman as an assistant gardener. This servant man had been instructed by the captain, as was the regular custom, to assume knowledge of some trade in order to secure a better situation. His deception was soon discovered by his master and an explanation demanded. On hearing the servant's story, the master sympathized with him and gave him an easy position in his household. The boy appeared well pleased with his situation for a time, but soon became discontented, neglectful, and finally ran away. He was discovered almost famished and returned to his master. The master, much angered by the ingratitude of the youth, determined to send him to the iron mines. The young man acknowledged the justice of the sentence, but pleaded that homesickness, gloom, and discontent had overcome all sense of gratitude. Touched by his misery, the master gave him his freedom and secured for him a position as steward on a ship about to sail for England. Two years later the master received from his former runaway servant a letter of thanks with an

---

[1] Letters from America, 1770, p. 68.

inclosure of £30.[2] The integrity of the servant and the conduct of the master in the account just given are doubtless rare exceptions, but it serves as a good example of the utter disappointment and despair which led many to desert their masters, regardless of the treatment they had received.

Outside of the convict class, by far the largest number of runaways came from the ranks of the outcasts, and "ne'er-do-wells" from the cities of England and Ireland. Many of them, fleeing from justice, or suffering from the pangs of hunger, were attracted by the glowing accounts given by the agents, and eagerly accepted this method of reaching the land of gold. It is not at all likely that these persons had any intention of fulfilling the conditions of the indenture, and thought only of the free transportation to America. These and the convicts became the professional runaways, who baffled all laws of the Assembly, and advertisements for whom occupy such a large space in the newspapers, making it appear that the whole servant body was continually running away. From the publication of the first newspaper in Maryland till long after the Revolution, it is difficult to find a number whose columns do not contain from one to ten advertisements for runaway servants and it is apparent from the descriptions given that they usually belonged to this class. I have counted as many as sixteen of these notices in a single issue of the Maryland Gazette (August 9, 1753). These advertisements for runaways throw much light upon various phases of servitude. Speedy apprehension depended to a great degree on accuracy of description of the person, his mannerisms, his clothing, his nationality, and other details which can be found in no other place. The following is a fair example of these newspaper notices. It does not give as minute a description of the person as many of them, but it shows how the size of the reward varied with the distance from home:

---

[2] Letters from America, pp. 78-79.

Fugitive Servants.

"RAN AWAY, from the subscriber, living on Monocacy, Carroll's Manor, in Frederick County, 6 miles from Frederick-Town, on the 27th of December last, *an indented Irish Servant Man* known by the name of *Patrick Quigley*, a Shoemaker by trade, of middling stature, well set, of ruddy complection, short black hair, about 5 feet 2 or 3 inches high, 24 years of age; had on and took with him when he absented a felt hat half worn, short blue sailor's jacket; red waistcoat, pair of white cloath breeches, a pair of white and a pair of black speckled milled stockings, and a pair of old shoes with steel buckles. Whoever takes up the Said Servant and brings him to the subscriber or secures him in any gaol, so that his master may get him again shall have, if taken 20 miles from home, TWENTY SHILLINGS; if 30 miles, THIRTY SHILLINGS; if a farther distance, THREE POUNDS, including what the law allows, and reasonable charges, if brought home to

DANIEL HARDMAN.

"January 8, 1785." [3]

These advertisements show that by far the greatest number of fugitives were Irish, and next in order came the English. In spite of the great numbers of German redemptioners that poured into Maryland in the latter part of the eighteenth and the first part of the nineteenth century, comparatively few notices of their running away appears in the papers. The few German fugitives which are met with after the Revolution may have been some of the Hessians who had been sent over as servants after being dismissed from the British army. Occasional notices of Welshmen, Frenchmen, Swedes, and even Jews are given among the runaways.

For the punishment and prevention of this wholesale running away very stringent laws were enacted by the General Assembly throughout the period. In March, 1641-2, an

---

[3] Md. Gazette and Balt. Adv. Jan. 25, 1785.

act was passed making it felony and punishable with death for a servant to depart secretly from his master or mistress with intent to convey himself out of the province.[4] This penalty might be commuted by the proprietor or the governor to servitude not exceeding seven years. Anyone who accompanied or assisted such a fugitive was subject to the same penalty as the fugitive himself.[5] This law was superseded by the act of April, 1649-50, which made it felony to assist a servant in running away, but the servant was required only to serve double the time of his absence and to pay all costs and damages by servitude. The same penalty was imposed upon hired servants, but those who assisted them were not guilty of felony and were required only to pay double damages and costs for the servant's absence.[6] It does not appear from a study of the court records that the death penalty, or even servitude for seven years, was ever imposed upon the servant or his accessory, although running away was frequent.

The colonies being practically independent of one another, servants escaping from one colony to another were secure unless the governor and council of that colony were willing to surrender them. The governors recognized the necessity of a mutual agreement upon the subject, and at an early date entered into negotiations for the return of all fugitives. In 1643, the Council of Maryland addressed a letter to the governor of New Netherlands stating that servants had fled from Maryland into New Netherlands, and requesting that they and all others who might in future be discovered be returned to the Maryland authorities. The Council promises to return any fugitives from New Netherlands who

---

[4] The death penalty, but with benefit of clergy, was imposed by a law of 1638-9 entitled An Act allowing brooke to certain Felonies. See chapter on Status.
[5] Arch. of Md. I. pp. 107-108; Bacon's Laws of Md. 1641, Ch. 6.
[6] Ibid. 249, 250. Those who assisted a freeman debtor to escape were also obliged to pay all damages caused by his absence. This last law was repealed by the act of 1676, Ch. 2 Bacon's Laws.

might flee into Maryland.⁷ The request was granted by New Netherlands, but this agreement, like nearly all the colonial laws, was not and could not always be enforced. In October, 1659, the governor of New Netherlands sent a very caustic letter to Maryland, complaining that many servants from his colony had gone into Maryland and "it is strongly suspected by means of . . . odious and injurious designs from hand to hand incouradged." He warns Maryland that unless she returns all fugitives to the South River, he will "publish free liberty acces and recess to all Planters Servants, Negroes, ffugitives and Runaways" from Maryland.⁸ The New Netherland government did its best to fulfill its part of the agreement, and rewards were offered to informers against those who harbored fugitives. Officers who allowed fugitives to escape from their custody were sometimes required to pay for goods that fugitives had stolen from their masters.⁹ Maryland made agreements for the return of fugitives with Pennsylvania and Virginia, and although private individuals sometimes tried to entice servants from other colonies, the provincial government did its best to discourage it. For example, two servants from Virginia supposed to belong to William Claiborne were taken up in March, 1656. The court ordered that the sheriff should immediately convey them to the Virginia border and turn them over to the proper officers.¹⁰ In the following year, two other fugitives from Virginia, one belonging to Nathaniel Bacon, were ordered by the court to be carried over the Potomac and delivered "into the Custody of Some of his Highness officers in Virginia." ¹¹

To frame laws far-reaching enough and stringent enough to prevent running away was a difficult matter. Not even

---

⁷ Arch of Md. III. pp.134-135.
⁸ Arch. of Md. III. p. 372.
⁹ Records of New Amsterdam 1653-74. Ed. by Fernow I. pp. 11, 12, 330, 331.
¹⁰ Arch. of Md. X. p. 442.
¹¹ Arch. of Md. X. pp. 515-516.

the liability of the death penalty or servitude for seven years sufficed to keep them from absconding. Another course had to be pursued. It was necessary to frame laws which would compel the fugitive when captured to repay his master for the expense incurred in his capture and the damages caused by his absence. Means must be devised for identifying fugitives. Rigid measures must be adopted to prevent freemen from assisting or concealing runaway servants and to compel them to reimburse the master with all damage caused by the absence of such servants as they had concealed or entertained.

If we except the laws of 1639 and 1641 which imposed the death penalty upon fugitives, there is very little difference in the various acts concerning runaways which were enacted throughout the entire period; therefore, no chronological account of them is necessary. The penalties for violating these laws were increased from time to time, but the laws themselves remain practically unchanged.

The most effective laws passed for the apprehension of fugitives were those concerning passes. They applied to both freemen and servants. Everyone traveling outside of his own county was required to carry a pass bearing the seal of the county where he resided, for which he must pay ten pounds of tobacco. If he had no pass and were not "Sufficiently known or able to give a good accompt of himself," he was considered a runaway and punished accordingly.[12] By the law of 1642, no one could obtain a pass unless he first posted notices of his intended departure at least five days before he wished to leave the country.[13] In 1666, the period for which such notices must be posted was raised to three months.[14] No servant, whether hired or indentured, was permitted to go ten miles from home with-

---

[12] Law of 1676, Arch. of Md. II. p. 524; Law of 1692, Ibid. XIII. p. 452; Law of 1715, Park's Laws, p. 107.
[13] Arch. of Md. I. p. 160.
[14] Ibid. II. pp. 145-146.

out a pass from his master or mistress.[15] The pass system, while a very effective instrument for preventing the escape of fugitives, was frequently a source of embarrassment to the freemen who had neglected to secure passes. All strangers were suspected as runaways. The Sot-Weed Factor relates that when he asked for lodging,

> "The surley Peasant bid me stay,
> And ask'd from whom I'de run away."

A study of the newspaper notices of runaways shows that even the pass laws did not always prove effective. The professional runaway was never at a loss for ways of evading them. Passes from masters were often counterfeited or old passes altered to suit the occasion. Several of these notices state that the fugitive carries a former indenture, which seems to have answered the same purpose as a pass. The penalty imposed by most laws was ten days' servitude for each day's absence. They were also required to repay the master, by servitude or otherwise, for all moneys expended in rewards, advertisements or other expenses connected with their capture. The servant, however, could always demand a hearing before the court, and the records show that where cruelty or neglect was found to be the real cause for running away that the penalties were not imposed and in some cases the servant was set free.

Throughout the history of servitude there were always those among the freemen who, either from humane motives or from a desire to secure the services of the servant themselves, did not hesitate to conceal the fugitive or assist him in his escape. To prevent this, anyone found guilty of assisting or entertaining a fugitive servant, knowing him to be such, was fined five hundred pounds of tobacco for every twenty-four hours' entertainment, and to make the law more effective the informer received half of the fine.[16]

---

[15] Laws of 1676 and 1715 cited above.
[16] By the law of 1666 the penalty was raised to 500 lbs. for the first night and 1,000 lbs. for the second. Arch. of Md. II. p. 146.

Fear of the laws not proving sufficient in all cases to prevent servants and others from breaking them, a system of rewards was adopted to encourage the planters to fulfill the requirements of the laws. Anyone apprehending a stranger who had no pass and could not give a satisfactory account of himself to the court was entitled to a reward of two hundred pounds of tobacco. If the suspect proved to be a servant, the reward was paid by his master and charged to the servant, who repaid it with extra servitude. If he were found to be a freeman, he must pay the reward himself or make satisfaction by servitude. Indians who apprehended a runaway and presented him before a magistrate received a Match coat or its value, the fugitives repaying the county by servitude or otherwise at the discretion of the judges. A standing reward of four hundred pounds of tobacco was offered to the inhabitants of Virginia, Delaware, and the northern colonies, who should arrest fugitives from Maryland and return them to any Maryland magistrate. The reward was paid out of the public assessment, and finally by the servant. Besides the rewards provided for by the laws, the masters usually offered an additional reward, the amount of which varied with the distance of the place of capture from the home of the master. A much larger reward was always offered for returning a servant who had fled into another province. This also was paid by the servant.[17]

All justices of the peace or commissioners before whom fugitives were brought were required to post notices in several conspicuous places, so that masters might know of the detention of their servants and claim them. No master of a ship was allowed to enter and trade in the ports of Maryland until he had taken an oath not to carry away or conceal any servant or slave belonging to any planter of the province. A violation of this law was punishable with a

---

[17] Eddis Letters, p. 71. See also newspapers.

fine of twenty shillings for every hour that the servant was concealed.[18]

In general, the laws against fugitives seem to have proved successful in preventing their escape. The pass system made detection an easy matter, and rewards to the informer encouraged every freeman and Indian to play the rôle of a private detective. The impassable rivers were another barrier to the successful flight of the servant. Very few bridges were then to be found, and anyone asking for transportation by boat was very likely to be asked for his pass. Eddis, writing in 1770, says that very few of the runaways succeeded in escaping.[19]

Many writers have adopted erroneous conclusions concerning servitude from confining their study, evidently, to laws alone. They have assumed that all possible abuses which might flow from these laws were actually practised upon the ignorant and defenceless servant. Fiske, for example, gives an entirely wrong impression when he speaks of servants in general as pasing "into a state of servitude which might be prolonged indefinitely by avaricious or cruel masters.[20] Such, however, was not and could not be the case in Maryland. No extension of the term of servitude could be made except by action of the court, and recorded cases show that the law was enforced. To be sure, the law during part of the period required the runaway to serve ten days for each day's absence, but it was "to be Judged when such master . . . shall bring the said servant before the Justices of the Provincial or County Court." [21] As another precaution against unjust extension of time, any indenture made with a servant during his term of servitude was declared void, and "shall not any wayes oblige any Servant for a longer tyme than by his first indenture."

---

[18] Bacon's Laws, 1753.
[19] Letters, pp. 70-71.
[20] Old Virginia and her Neighbors, II. p. 177.
[21] Law of 1676 Arch. of Md. II. p. 524. See also Law of 1715, Park's Laws of Md. p. 107.

The court proceedings contain a sufficient number of cases to give us a good idea of the treatment of runaway servants. Sometimes it was found that the servant had been brutally treated by the master or was not properly cared for; but quite often the servant was clearly in the wrong. The court always gave the fugitive a hearing, and, by the examination of witnesses, endeavored to determine the merits of the claims of the contending parties. Where it was proved that the servant had run away without sufficient reason he was required to serve extra time, but generally not to the full limit of the law. If, on the other hand, it was found that the master had cruelly treated the servant he was punished and, in some cases, the servant set free. The following cases will give a fair idea of the treatment of runaways by the courts of Maryland. In St. Mary's court, July 16, 1654, Richard Wells entered a complaint against two of his servants for "Carelessly absenting themselves for a Long time from his Service." The servants alleged abuse in giving them correction. After an investigation the court decided that the correction was "not given without just cause" and the servants' time was extended eight months to repay the master for damage sustained and for 200 pounds of tobacco which it had cost him for sheriff and court charges.[22]

At a court held on Kent Island in August, 1652, Thomas Ward was fined 300 pounds of tobacco for cruelly beating his runaway servant.[23] The case of Susan Frizell, April, 1655, affords evidence that sympathy for the servant class was not entirely wanting among the planters. Susan was convicted for absenting herself from her master's service for three weeks. She was sentenced to serve double the time of her absence and to pay fifty pounds of tobacco damage. She complained of harsh usage and said she was afraid to return to her master. The court set her free on

---

[22] Arch. of Md. X. p. 396.
[23] Hanson, Old Kent of Md. p. 23.

condition that she would pay to her master 500 pounds of tobacco after the next crop to reimburse him for what she had cost him. The bystanders immediately subscribed 600 pounds for her which more than paid for release.[24]

Runaways were sometimes subjected to corporal punishment instead of extra servitude and where several entered into a conspiracy to run away the court often remitted the punishment of those enticed into the plot on condition that they would administer the prescribed number of lashes to the guilty ones.[25] Whether the verdict of the court was in favor of the fugitive or against him it was never rendered without deliberation and the examination of witnesses. Sworn testimony in the various suits recorded nearly always warrant the decision of the court, and as petitions from servants were always received and considered by the judges, there could be no indiscriminate extension of the term of servitude at the will of the master.

---

[24] Arch. of Md. X. p. 416.
[25] Ibid. pp. 511, 512, 513, 514, 517.

CHAPTER VI.

STATUS OF SERVANTS AND FREEDMEN.

A careful study of the laws connected with white servitude and an examination of their application by the courts gives, on the whole, a more favorable idea of the legal and social status of the servant and freedman than is usually found in histories dealing with this matter.

Most historians have treated the subject in a very cursory manner and for that reason have given us a rather distorted idea of the institution. In nearly every case they have selected the most severe laws and the most barbarous cases of treatment and given these as a representation of servitude in all places and at all times. Laws for the protection of the servant and their enforcement by the courts; instances of indulgence and kindness on the part of the master are rarely mentioned.

To condemn the entire system because of the actions of the law breakers of the time is hardly more just than to judge our own state of civilization by the numerous murders and other crimes that are daily committed in our midst. Like all other systems of bondage this had a tendency to develop the brutal nature of both master and servant, but a careful study of the institution reveals much that is good as well as much evil.

To form a correct idea of the status of the servant we must use as a standard the status of the freeman of the same period. The history of white servitude records many customs and abuses that are revolting in the extreme; however, as compared with freemen the position of servants in the early years of the colony was much better than in later years. The Palatines and other German races, who in the later years formed nearly all of the servant population, knew little of the laws and language and were an easy prey to the abuses of traders and harsh masters. They had been used to very little liberty at home and were slow to assert their rights in America.

At no time in the history of Maryland was the condition of the servant that of a slave. He always possessed rights which must be respected and which were generally enforced by the courts. He was free to bring cases before the courts, to summon witnesses, and to demand a jury trial. As soon as his indenture or term by custom had expired he at once became a freeman with all the rights of a British subject. In the early years of the colony, freedmen entered the Assembly and no doubt had no little influence in framing the laws in favor of the servant. By a comparison of the lists of imported servants given by Neill [1] with the lists of members of the Assemblies, we find that in the Assembly of 1637-38 there were fifteen former servants. There was also another who had been a servant of Claibourne and Clobery but who had purchased his freedom for a yearly payment of 300 pounds of tobacco when Evelin took control of Kent Island.[2] In the same manner we find that in 1642 there were thirteen freedmen either present in the Assembly, excused for absence or fined for non-appearance. Other instances are found in later Assemblies of the presence of freed servants. Cuthbert Fenwick, although brought in as a servant by Captain Cornwallis, became the latter's attorney and one of the most prominent men in the colony as well as a member of several assemblies.[3]

The first courts of Maryland were erected by the Assembly of 1638-39.[4] Among the offences to be determined by

---

[1] Founders of Md.
[2] Streeter Papers, p. 25, *note*.
[3] Freedmen were also elected to the House of Burgesses of Virginia.—Fiske, Old Virginia and her Neighbors, II. 186. Servants in Massachusetts while under indenture were given the elective franchise during the first sixteen years of the settlement. Hurd, Laws of Freedom and Bondage, I. p. 255.
[4] Arch. of Md. I. pp. 46-49.

the Lieutenant-General, by any one of the council, or by the Justice of the Peace was the ill treatment of servants by their masters. Any master refusing to provide sufficient food and clothing for his servant or neglecting to fulfill the contract for wages, etc., was to be imprisoned until he gave security to perform the order of the judge. For a second offence the indenture was to be cancelled and the servant set free. Masters were forbidden to work their servants on the Sabbath or any other holy day under penalty of thirty pounds of tobacco or five shillings sterling for each offence. Servants not performing their part of the contract were to be whipped or otherwise corrected at the discretion of the court.[5] In the records of this Assembly is found the first mention of a law which is the most severe of all laws against the servant. Among the crimes enumerated as felonies are manslaughter, arson, forgery, etc., and "Stealth of ones self which is the unlawful departure of a Servant out of service or out of the Colony without the privity or Consent of the Master or Mistresse." The penalty for each of these offences is fixed at "death by hanging except the offender can read clerk like in the judgment of the court.[6] The Assembly of 1641 also made running away felony and punishable with death, but here again it was provided that the proprietor or the governor "shall at the request of the partie so condemned exchange such pains of death into Servitude" and that "such exchange shall not exceed the time of Seven years."[7] Thus the death penalty for fugitives so often quoted as an example of barbarism really resolves itself into an extended servitude.

A study of actual court cases gives us a far better idea of legal status of the servant than a mere perusal of the laws. The prominence of the master seems not in any case to have affected the legal protection of the servant. In May,

---

[5] Arch. of Md. I. p. 53.
[6] Ibid. p. 72.
[7] Ibid. pp. 107-108.

1644, William Harrington recovered 1,525 pounds of tobacco from Leonard Calvert as custom dues for four years' service.[8] In January, 1656-67, a servant, Henry Billsbury, complained in the Patuxent court that his master, John Little, had cruelly treated him. The court ordered the sheriff to accompany the servant to his home and require the master to give bond for good treatment of the servant and for the master's appearance at the next court to answer to the charges brought against him by the servant. If the master should refuse to give such bond the servant was to be taken from him and the master was to remain in custody of the sheriff till the bond were given.[9] In 1652, Mark Benton, servant of Robert Vaughan, commander of Kent Island, petitioned the court for his "freedom with corne and clothes." The court decided in his favor.[10] At the December court of Kent Island, 1652, Thomas Weest, servant of Henry Morgan, gentleman and one of the commissioners of Kent Island, was allowed "his freedom and freedom corn with whatever besides may be usual according to the custom of the country." [11] In this suit the claim of the servant was evidently not proved to the entire satisfaction of the court as the master was given a certain time in which to produce the indenture but the servant was given the benefit of the doubt.

Sometimes the servant was hired out by his master to another planter, in which case the employer was responsible for the food, clothing and proper treatment of the servant. In the October term of the provincial court, Simon Bird, a servant who had been hired to Robert Taylor, complained that he had not been provided with necessary clothing "which complaint appeareth to this Court to have Sufficient ground." The court ordered Taylor to properly clothe the

---

[8] Arch. of Md. IV. p. 271.
[9] Ibid. X. p. 474.
[10] Hanson, Old Kent of Maryland, pp. 21 and 28.
[11] Ibid. pp. 24, 28.

servant, and the commissioner was authorized to see that the order should be carried out.[12]

The testimony in these trials sometimes exposes extreme cruelty on the part of the masters. In the September court, 1657, a servant William Ireland complained that his master, Captain Morgan, inhumanly beat him and compelled him and the rest of the servants to prepare their own food at night after their day's work. He also alleged that they were often without sufficient food. The court forbade the master to beat his servant "unlawfully" or to work any of his servants at night unless in case of necessity.[13] No penalty was imposed in this case and it was probably the first offence.

Another revolting case of cruelty came before the Kent county court, September 28, 1674. William Drake, a servant of John Wells, complained that "your petitioner's master have several times abused by giving me unlawful correction, by tying my two handwrists together, hanging me up to ye gunne racks, and whipped me without mercy giving me at least one hundred blows upon my bare skin, and let me hang so long yt ye blood started through and out of my fingers and all my hands pealed, and his chiefest ayme was to strike me upon my members, when he was whipping me. After he commanded me to goe with him into ye wood along with him; which I did accordingly, to his desire, and when he had me there he was so unmerciful in beating of me, that he broke a hycory stick all in pieces—several other matters I could alege, but loth to be tedious." [14] Unfortunately the action of the court is not given in the records. This is an extreme case, and very few like it are found in the records of the court. Even the worst treatment recorded will compare quite favorably with the treatment

---

[12] Arch. of Md. X. p. 401.
[13] Ibid. p. 521.
[14] Hanson's Old Kent of Md. p. 223.

of some of the apprentices in England during the same period.[15]

It is stated by Fiske that the lives of servants were protected in theory only.[16] The records of Maryland contradict this statement as applying to that colony. Several cases of inquest over dead servants are given in the records of the seventeenth century. The master was not always found guilty of murder, neither did the evidence warrant such a verdict. In the Kent county court, August, 1652, Thomas Ward was tried for causing the death of his servant by whipping. After an investigation the jury found that death was due to other causes, but the master was fined 300 pounds of tobacco for "unreasonable and unchristianlike punishment" of the servant.[17] In the same court an inquest was held over the body of a Scotch servant, James Wilson. Upon investigation it was found that the servant died of fever and dropsy.[18] But the charges of murder were not always without foundation. On October 3, 1657, John Danby was executed for causing the death of one of his servants.[19] Other examples might be given to show that the lives of the servants were protected in practice as well

---

[15] The following is an example taken from the court records of October, 1655. Complaint was entered against the master that he required the apprentice to labor on the Sabbath and "that the said master did very much misuse his said apprentice by fasteninge of a lock with a chaine to it, and tyinge and fetteringe him to the shoppe, and that the said master his wife and mother did most cruelly and inhumanely beate his said apprentice, and also whip'd him until he was very blooddy and his flesh rawe over a great part of his body, and then salted him, and held him naked to the fyre, beinge soe salted to add to his paine."—Middlesex Co. Records, III. p. 239.
[16] "Their lives were in theory protected by law, but where an indented servant came to his death from prolonged ill usage, or from excessive punishment, or even from sudden violence, it was not easy to get a verdict against the master." Old Virginia and her Neighbors, III. p. 178.
[17] Hanson, Old Kent of Maryland, pp. 22-23.
[18] Ibid.
[19] Arch. of Md. X. pp. 535-545. The trial is recorded in full and gives a very good idea of a criminal trial in colonial times.

as in theory; that investigations of sudden deaths were made and the master punished, if guilty.

The decisions of the court of course were not always in favor of the servants. Sometimes they were ordered to serve extra time; and punishment of servants which we would now think very severe was often declared "not administered without just cause." But the records, on the whole, justify the statement of Hammond [20] that "Servants complaints are freely harkened to, and (if not carelessly made) their Masters are compelled either speedily to amend, or they are removed upon second complaint to another service; and often times not onely set free (if the abuse merit it) but ordered to give reparation and damage to their servant."

The regular punishment inflicted upon servants by the courts for offences other than running away was whipping upon the bare back. This followed very naturally from their pecuniary circumstances. They were presumed not to possess property, hence whipping was the only penalty which could be inflicted. This punishment, however, was not restricted to servants, but was administered to freemen for certain offences[21] or in default of payment of a fine.[22] The number of lashes varied from ten to thirty, according to the offence. At Patuxent Court, March 21, 1655-56, a servant was sentenced to ten "Slashes" because he "Scandalously abused his master." [23] Twenty lashes were sometimes ordered for servants who had forged passes." [24] None but hired servants were allowed to trade without consent of their masters.[25] The first law forbidding

---

[20] Leah and Rachell, p. 16.
[21] Arch. of Md. X. p. 558 and passim.
[22] Laws of 1663 and 1715 on trading with servants. See Park's Laws of Md. pp. 109, 110, and Arch. I. p. 500.
[23] Arch. of Md. X. pp. 439-440.
[24] Ibid. pp. 516-517.
[25] The privilege of trading without consent of the master was taken from hired servants by the law of 1715.—Park's Compleat Col. of Laws of Md.; Bacon's Laws of Md. 1715, Ch. 44.

them to trade was passed in 1663,[26] and similar laws were enacted from time to time throughout the period. This was an entirely just law, as very few servants, unless working for wages, had anything to sell without stealing it from their masters. Illicit traffic with servants seems to have been carried on to a great extent by seamen, and the penalty for violating this law was made very severe. Buying goods of a servant without the consent of his master was punishable with a fine of 2000 pounds of tobacco. If the defendant were unable to pay the fine, he must either give security for the amount or submit to thirty stripes on the bare back. The servant for the first offence was punished with thirty stripes; for the second offence, the same, and in addition was branded with a hot iron. It was ordered that a copy of this act should be posted on the mast of every ship to bar the plea of ignorance on the part of seamen.

The best of laws may sometimes be used by individuals in a way never intended by the framers. In fact, they may even promote the evils which they were enacted to prevent. Such a law was passed by the Maryland Assembly in September, 1664, and from it arose some very interesting cases and very important legal decisions. Among the servants imported into the colony, there were often women of a very low type, who during their term of servitude intermarried with negro slaves. Such marriages aroused the indignation of the better class of inhabitants, who considered the negro far more degraded than the vilest convict from Old Bailey or Newgate. Many disputes had also arisen concerning the status of the children born of such marriages. The penalties provided by the law of 1664 were thought to be severe enough to prevent any white woman from disgracing herself and society by contracting such a marriage in future. The preamble of the law states that "divers freeborne English women forgettful of their free condition and

---

[26] Arch. of Md. I. pp. 500-501.

to the disgrace of the Nation doe intermarry with Negro Slaves by which alsoe divers suites may arise touching the Issue of such women and a great damage doth befall the Masters." The punishment was made very severe for the purpose of "deterring such freeborne women from such shamefull Matches." [27] By this law any free-born woman contracting marriage with a slave was required to serve her master during the life of her husband. All children born to them were made slaves for life. Children of white women already married to slaves were to serve till thirty years of age. "This law," says Hennighausen, "was in violation of the ancient maxim, that the children of a free woman, the father being a slave, follow the status of their mother and are free." [28]

Instead of preventing such marriages, this law enabled avaricious and unprincipled masters to convert many of their servants into slaves. While this act continued in force, it did more to lower the standard of servitude than any other law passed during the whole period.

A very interesting case came up which brought about the repeal of the law of 1681. Among the servants brought over by Lord Baltimore was one named Eleanor, who later became famous in the court records as "Irish Nell." When Baltimore returned to England, he sold her to a planter, who soon married her to a negro slave named Butler. When Baltimore learned of this, he used his influence in securing the repeal of the law,[29] but as Nell was married while the law was in force she and her children were held as slaves. Nearly a century later,—September, 1770 [30]—William and Mary Butler, descendants of Irish Nell, petitioned the court for freedom on the ground that they had descended from a white woman. The Provincial Court

---

[27] Arch. of Md. I. pp. 533-534.
[28] The Redemptioners, p. 2.
[29] Harris and McHenry's Reports, I. p. 376.
[30] Wrongly given as 1721 by Hennighausen, p. 5.

granted them freedom,[31] but the Court of Appeals reversed the decision on the ground that Nell was a slave before the passage of the act of 1681. Once more the case was revived in 1787, when Mary Butler, daughter of William and Mary, petitioned for freedom. This time the slave was successful, both courts deciding in her favor.[32]

The repealing law was passed in September, 1681, and the preamble states that the marriage of white women with slaves was often due to the "Instigacon, Procuremt or Conievance" of the masters. It was, therefore, enacted that any master who "shall by any Instigacion procuremt knowledge permision or contrievance whatsoever, suffer any such ffreeborne Englishe or Whitewoman Servt in theire possession . . . to Intermarry . . . with any Slave . . . the same Mr Mi^{rs} or dame . . . shall forfeit & Loose all theire Claime & Title to the service and servitude of any such ffreeborne woman." Every such woman was by this act "absolutely discharged manymitted and made free Instantly upon her Intermarriage" with a slave.[33] All children of a woman so marrying were also made free. As an additional penalty, the master for each offence was to pay a fine of 10,000 pounds of tobacco. Priests and ministers were forbidden to join such couples in marriage, under a like penalty of 10,000 pounds of tobacco.

While this law very effectually protected the servant from evil designs of an avaricious master, it did not prevent lewd conduct on the part of the servant. Mingling of the races continued during the eighteenth century, in spite of all laws against it. Preventing marriages of white servants with

---

[31] Harris and McHenry, I. pp. 374, 376.
[32] Ibid. II. p. 214. The ground taken by the court was (1) The act of 1664 provided for no manner of trial for the offence. (2) There was no proof that Irish Nell was ever convicted of the offence in a court, a privilege to which every British subject is entitled. Ibid. p. 233. In 1782, a similar case came before the courts. Freedom was granted to Eleanor Toogood whose mother had been adjudged a slave for marrying a negro slave. Ibid. pp. 26, 38.
[33] Arch. of Md. VII. pp. 203-204.

slaves only led to a greater social evil, which caused a reaction of public sentiment against the servant. Masters and society in general were burdened with the care of illegitimate mulatto children, and it became necessary to frame laws compelling the guilty parties to reimburse the masters for the maintenance of these unfortunate waifs. By the laws of 1715 and 1717, any white man or white woman, who cohabited with a negro, free or slave, was made a servant for seven years and the children were made servants for thirty-one years. Masters were compelled by law to maintain bastard children of their women servants. If the father could be found, he was held responsible for the support of the child; if not, the mother must repay the master by servitude or otherwise.[34] This prevented illegitimate children from becoming a burden to the parishes as they were in Virginia.[35]

While the law of 1715 imposed a heavy penalty upon servants for transgressing the moral law, it also afforded them adequate legal protection from unjust treatment by their masters. Any master who refused to give the servant his freedom dues was required to pay a fine of 500 pounds of tobacco. If the servant were overworked, severely punished, deprived of necessary rest, or if he were not properly fed and clothed, the master was liable to a fine not exceeding 4000 pounds of tobacco. For the third offence the servant was set free. These acts, as a rule, were very well enforced.

Whipping as a punishment for servants seems to have gradually died out during the early part of the eighteenth century and fines were substituted instead. As neither fines nor costs could be collected from the servant, it was necessary to make the master responsible for the payment.

As the convict element increased in the colony and the

---

[34] Act of Assembly, Oct. 1727.
[35] Bishop Meade, Old Churches and Families of Virginia, I. p. 366.

servant class became more degraded, crimes and misdemeanors were frequent. Masters, knowing that the expense of prosecution must be borne by the county, did little to restrain their servants, unless their own interests were involved, and sometimes even encouraged them to commit petty crimes. The newspapers record many thefts and burglaries committed by convict servants. The cost of prosecuting so many culprits was no small item to the county. In 1727, the master was made responsible for all costs which might arise from the prosecution of his servant, and the servant was compelled to repay the master by extra servitude.[36] All necessity for inflicting corporal punishment upon the servant was finally removed by the law of 1750 which required the master to pay all fines, the servant repaying the amount by extended term.[37]

The legal status of the convicts was the same as that of all other servants, except in a few particulars. They, like the Catholics, were not subject to military duty, although some were enlisted during the French and Indian War.[38] Before 1751, their oath was not accepted in court. In that year, their testimony against other convicts was made legal.[39] Permission to testify in other causes was extended to most convicts in 1789. The General Court ruled that no convict could be disqualified as a witness unless it were clearly proved that he had been transported "for some offence made felony or infamous by the common law of England or by some Statute of Great Britain." [40] As this could rarely be done, all legal disabillity was practically removed from the convict servant.

The social position of the servant is a matter which cannot easily be determined. Contemporaries usually tell us

---

[36] Acts of Assembly, 1727, pp. 6, 7.
[37] Bacon's Laws for May 15, 1750, Ch. 5, Sec. 2.
[38] Sharpe to Lords of Trade, Feb. 8, 1756. Arch. of Md. VI. p. 353.
[39] Bacon's Laws of Md. 1751, Chap. 11; continued, 1763, Ch. 19; June 1773, Ch. 2; and Oct. 1780, Ch. 12, Green's Laws of Md.
[40] Harris and McHenry's Reports, II. p. 380.

of the two extremes according to the object they had in view. Some, like Alsop, whose business it was to encourage immigration, would have us believe that the servant's station was an enviable one. Others, like Eddis and Fearon, represent the life of a servant as worse than that of the slave. A middle ground seems to be nearer the truth. It is quite probable that in the early years of the colony the servant differed little socially from the master whom he served. Both were ignorant and lived the "happy-go-lucky" life of the frontiersman and cared little for the morrow.[41] Illiteracy is everywhere noticeable in the records. In a list of names of Kent islanders who pledged their loyalty to the Commonwealth in 1652, 31 out of 66 signed with their mark.[42] Many masters themselves were only freed servants. Servants often married into the families of their masters, and many who did not were treated as members of the family. As society advanced the position of the servant did not advance with it, but rather deteriorated. The large importation of convicts and fugitives from justice and the mingling of servants with slaves tended to degrade the whole servant class. Eben Cook in his Sot-weed Factor gives a graphic description of this class of immigrants:

> "Who when they cou'd not live at Home,
> For refuge to these Worlds did roam;
> In hopes by Flight they might prevent
> The Devil and his fell intent;
> Obtained from Tripple-Tree reprieve,
> And Heav'n and Hell alike deceive."

An apparently reliable account of servitude in the middle of the seventeenth century is given by Hammond in his account of Virginia and Maryland. He gives both the good and the evil of the system and nearly all his statements are borne out by the records. He warns the immigrants not to be deceived by the agents, to have a contract in writing, and

---

[41] Mayer, Groundrents in Maryland, App. p. 137.
[42] Hanson, Old Kent of Md. pp. 59-60.

to come as freemen if possible.[43] On the whole, he gives a very favorable account of servitude as he saw it in 1656. "The labour servants are put to is not so hard nor of such continuance as Husbandmen, nor Handicraft are kept at in England. I said little or nothing is done in winter time, none ever work before sunrise nor after sunset, in the summer they rest, sleep or exercise themselves five houres in the heat of the day. Saturdays afternoon is always their own, the old Holidayes are observed and the Sabbath spent in good exercise." This corresponds in the main with Alsop's account written ten years later.[44] Whether or not it was the custom to allow servants Saturday afternoon we cannot say, but it could not legally be claimed by the servant.[45] It is quite probable that it was usually allowed by the masters, for even those working for wages claimed it as a privilege.[46] Only the worst class of women, says Hammond, were compelled to labor in the fields.[47] Servants were comfortably housed and fed, and when they performed their duties faithfully were usually given some ground to plant and cattle to raise for their own use. The property thus accumulated together with the freedom dues enabled an industrious servant to become at once a planter upon the expiration of his servitude.

Later writers give us an etirely different picture of servant life from that given by Hammond and Alsop. The Labadists, Danker and Sluyter, who traveled in Maryland in 1679 were loud in their denunciation of servitude. "For their usual food the servants have nothing but maise bread to eat and water to drink which sometimes is not very good and scarcely enough for life, yet they are compelled to work hard . . . and thus they are by hundreds of thousands

---

[43] Leah and Rachell, pp. 10, 11, 12 in Force's Tracts, Vol. III.
[44] Character of the Province of Md. p. 57.
[45] Arch. of Md. I. p. 21.
[46] Arch. of Md. I. p. 306.
[47] Leah and Rachell, pp. 12, 14. This was not so in the eighteenth century as women regularly worked on tobacco plantations.

(sic) compelled to spend their lives here and in Virginia, and elsewhere in planting that vile tobacco, which all vanishes into smoke, and is for the most part miserably abused."[48] This account comes from foreigners and moralists and no doubt represents the very worst side of servitude. In the same narrative we are told that "the servants and negroes, after they have worn themselves down the whole day and gone home to rest, have yet to grind and pound the grain, which is generally maise, for their masters and all their families as well as themselves and all the negroes to eat." The account continues with a rather improbable story of cruelty," a master having a sick servant, and there are many so, and observing from his declining condition, he would finally die, and that there was no probability of his enjoying any more service from him, made him, sick and languishing as he was, dig his own grave, in which he was laid a few days afterwards, the others being too busy to dig it, having their hands full in attending to the tobacco." But the condition of the planters as described by the same writers was little above that of the servant from either a material or a moral standpoint. They subsisted entirely on the same maise bread which the writers pronounced "miserable. Milk and butter were luxuries never indulged in. Their lives were "godless and profane. They listen neither to God nor his commandments, and have neither church nor cloister." What ministers they had were "worse than anybody else." When a ship arrived with liquor on board the planters flocked round it, not leaving it till either their money or the liquor was gone. Nothing was brought home for the use of the family, although they were often without the necessaries of life.[49] It is with this state of society that we must compare the social status of the servant of the same period.

Eddis, another foreigner, writing nearly a century later

---

[48] Voyage to N. Y. Mem. of L. I. Hist. Soc. I. p. 192.
[49] Voyage to N. Y. Mem. of L. I. Hist. Soc. I. pp. 217, 218.

(1770) adds a word of condemnation of the system of white servitude. Servants and convicts, according to his account, were treated alike and both fared worse than the slave. The planters considered themselves in the light of penitentiary wardens carrying out the sentence of the British courts. "They are strained to the utmost to perform their allotted labour; and, from a prepossession in many cases too justly founded, they are supposed to be receiving only the just reward which is due to repeated offences."[50] "There are doubtless many exceptions," he adds, "yet, generally speaking, they groan beneath a worse than Egyptian bondage." This account, as applying to some masters, is doubtless true, but it represents only the darkest side of the system. Even at its worst it was better than languishing in a debtor's cell in England. A little more than a decade before this we are told that "about 25,000 of the most useful Subjects are locked up in Gaols or forced to abscond."[51]

Several causes combined to degrade the condition of servants in Maryland in the years which immediately preceded and followed the Revolution. After the treaty of Utrecht in 1713, English vessels began importing slaves in greater numbers than ever before, and by the middle of the century the slave element in Maryland had considerably increased.[52] There were not, however, a sufficient number of slaves to cultivate the plantations and servants were regularly employed along with slaves in the cultivation of tobacco.

By 1770, Maryland was the only colony which had not succeeded in practically excluding convicts,[53] and they continued to come to Annapolis and Baltimore in large numbers. The constant association of servants with convicts and slaves had a demoralizing effect upon them and in-

---

[50] Eddis Letters, pp. 69, 70.
[51] London Chronicle, May, 1757, p. 500.
[52] In 1748, there were 36,000 slaves to 94,000 whites; 1770, 59,717 slaves to 140,100 whites; and in 1790, 103,036 slaves to 208,649 whites. Kennedy, Hist. and Statistics of Md. p. 19.
[53] Eddis Letters, p. 66.

creased the severity of their treatment. They labored side by side, the servant for a term of years, the slave for life, and the tendency was for many masters to treat them all alike. Maryland depended largely upon servant schoolmasters for the instruction of youth. "At least two-thirds of the little education we receive," says Boucher, "are derived from instructors, who are either *indented servants* or *transported felons*."[54] This was not a random statement, but was made after an investigation of the subject. Concerning the character of these servant schoolmasters, there is little said by other contemporaries.

The German redemptioners who continued to pour into Maryland long after the Revolution were an honest and industrious people, and did much toward developing the country. Their peaceable dispositions, while often exposing them to indignities from both slaves and masters,[55] made them more valuable servants than those from other countries. An editorial in the Maryland Journal gives testimony of their high character and industry. "It has been generally allowed that the German emigrants were formerly remarkable, at least the major part of them, for their integrity and industry, which give them the preference as Servants, before any other nation."[56] This standard was lowered somewhat by the importation of Hessians who had served in the British army during the American Revolution and who brought with them all the vices of camp life.[57] Frances Wright, who visited the United States in 1818-20 and who took a special interest in the immigrants of that

---

[54] View of Causes and Consequences of the Am. Rev. pp. 183-184.
[55] "The natural cunning of the Negro, his superior dexterity, and fluency in English give him too great an advantage over the simple, good-natured German peasant. He considers himself as of a higher nature and looks down upon the poor German. The latter is confounded in treatment with the blacks, nay is often treated worse. Fürstenwärther, Der Deusche in Nord-Amerika, p. 55, quoted by Everett in N. Am. Rev. 1820, Vol. 2, p. 10.
[56] Md. Jour. and Balt. Adv. Apr. 15, 1785.
[57] Ibid.

period, has left a very good account of the relative merits of immigrants from the several countries. "The starving emigrants of Switzerland and Germany are simple agriculturists and ignorant peasants who here quietly devote themselves to the pursuits from which they have been driven in Europe, and instantly become harmless and industrious citizens. Their prejudices, whatever they might be, are perfectly innocent, and of absolute vices they usually have none."[58] The Welsh, in general, resembled the Germans, and made valuable servants. The English and Irish came usually from the cities, and were not fitted for the labor required of servants. "An Englishman, in general," says the author, "can do but one thing, and an Irishman, but too frequently, can do nothing."

Many of the injustices experienced by the German and Swiss redemptioners were removed by the exertions of the German Society of Maryland, which was incorporated in February, 1817. Its object, as stated elsewhere, was primarily to prevent abuses on shipboard, but it also did much to better the condition of servants on land. As the Germans were unable to speak our language, they might be induced to sign an indenture without knowing its significance. By the law of 1817, instigated by the German Society, no indenture or contract was valid unless made out or sanctioned by the officer appointed for that purpose, who must be familiar with both languages. All indentures were registered and filed at the county courts in order to prevent unjust claims of the masters. The term of servitude was again reduced to four years for adults. No minor could be indentured without the consent of his parents or nearest living relative, and could in no case be bound to serve for a term extending beyond majority. But a still greater step toward social uplifting of these poor immigrants was the provision that every indenture must contain a clause re-

---

[58] Views of America, p. 430.

quiring the master to give every minor servant at least two months' schooling each year.[59] Armed with this law, the German Society at once set to work to rigidly carry it into operation. They did much to better the condition of the servant by legal protection and pecuniary assistance.[60] The officers frequently found cases where servants were ill-treated. On the other hand, many complaints were unfounded and caused in the main by some misunderstanding or by misconduct of the servant. The president of the society to whom the complaints were usually made laments that "the want of understanding the language is frequently the occasion of injustice on the part of the master, and more frequently of his agents and the impropriety of conduct on the part of the servant."

Having traced the institution of servitude through the two hundred years of its existence, it has been found that, on the whole, the legal protection of the servant was adequate and usually carried into effect. Their social position, which for many years differed little from that of the freemen of the time, gradually deteriorated with the increase of convicts and the growth of slavery.

The status of the freedman is more difficult to trace, but, in general, there was a downward movement, as in the case of the servant. Legally, the freedman at all times enjoyed the privileges of a freeman. Socially, this was not always the case. In the early years of the colony, when land was abundant and the proprietor did everything in his power to develop the province and increase his rent roll, the freed servant at once became a prosperous planter, and the fact that he had been a servant was soon forgotten. So large a proportion of the immigrants came over in this way that servitude carried with it no disgrace. Later on, land was harder to obtain, and the servants, except the Germans, were a more worthless class. When set free, they helped

---

[59] Laws of Md. Dec. Sess. 1817, pp. 224-226.
[60] See Henninghausen, The Redemptioners, pp. 14 ff.

to swell the ranks of the class known as white trash." [61]

Some of the freedmen and their descendants in Maryland and other colonies rose to prominence. Daniel Dulany, the elder, one of Maryland's greatest lawyers, was an Irish indentured servant.[62] The parents of Major General Sullivan were redemptioners.[63] Others of national reputation had themselves been servants. Among them were George Taylor [64] and Matthew Thornton, signers of the Declaration of Independence; also Charles Thomson, secretary of congress during the Revolution.[65] Mathew Lyon, the "Hampden of Congress," was a kidnapped servant.[66]

---

[61] Fiske, Old Virginia and her Neighbors, II. pp. 188-189.
[62] Boyle, Biographical Sketches of Distinguished Marylanders, p. 35. Sioussat, Public Services of Daniel Dulany, J. H. U. Stud. Series XXI. No. 8.
[63] Scharf, Hist. of Md. I. p. 373.
[64] McLaughlin's Mathew Lyon, p. 40, *note*.
[65] Scharf I. p. 373.
[66] McLaughlin's Mathew Lyon, p. 34 ff.

CHAPTER VII.

SERVANT MILITIA.

In Maryland, as in other colonies, servants were required to perform military duty in defending themselves and others from the attacks of the Indians.

It was always a much-disputed question whether the government had a right to impair the contract between master and servant by impressing the latter into the army. In the early years of the colony no provision was made by the Assembly for supplying the army with food and munitions of war, and the expenses of a campaign were borne by the individual planters.

During the first fifty years, the planters do not appear to have denied the right of the government to enlist the servants, but they considered it a great burden to be obliged to equip a large number of servants for war, and very often they neglected or refused to comply with the laws.

For a number of years the servants formed a large proportion of the able-bodied men in the colony and were of considerable importance from a military standpoint. As the greater number had been brought from Europe, more on account of the land received for their transportation than from the profit resulting from their labor, the time lost by the servant in military operation was no serious loss to his master, and had the expense been borne by the Assembly the servant might have enlisted without opposition. Although the planters often neglected to equip their servants with arms, it was not till tobacco and wheat growing became a profitable enterprise and the servants' labor indispensable, and when the king or the governor demanded military duty of the servant in wars which were distasteful or viewed with indifference by the colonists, that both the economic and the military importance of the servant was realized and the strife over the right of the king or the colony to impress the servant began.

As early as 1638-39, the Assembly passed a law, entitled "An act for Military Discipline."[1] It required every householder to have ready on all occasions for himself and every person in his house, able to bear arms—which included servants—a serviceable gun and a prescribed amount of ammunition. As soon as any alarm was given, he must send one man completely armed for every three in his household. All expenses were to be borne by the master.

A new law was passed in April, 1649, which imposed a penalty of 100 pounds of tobacco for neglecting to furnish necessary arms for servants. Masters were ordered to equip all hired servants and to deduct the amount from their wages.[2]

The records concerning military affairs in the early years are scanty, but there is an occasional mention of servants being pressed into service. At the court held at St. Mary's November 25, 1652, to consider the raising of troops for an expedition against the Indians, it was required that every six persons in the province should equip a seventh with food and ammunition for the campaign. In making up the list it was ordered "that William Thompson Servant to John Jarbo of St. Maries County be pressed for one of the Seventh men in the County."[3]

It was a difficult matter to compel masters to provide arms for their servants, and, in 1654, the officers in each county were ordered by the Assembly to inspect every household and see that each servant between sixteen and sixty years of age was provided with arms and ammunition. The officers were also authorized to drill the servants for duty.[4] Masters

---

[1] Arch. of Md. I. pp. 77-78.
[2] Ibid. pp. 254-255.
[3] Arch. of Md. III. p. 283.
[4] Ibid. p. 347.

not only neglected to equip their servants, but many refused to allow them to drill or perform other military duty. In 1661, officers were authorized to enlist as many persons between sixteen and sixty years as they saw fit. It was further provided that "in case any of the aforesaid Officers shall happen to enlist any Servant . . . and that their Master . . . shall refuse to lett such Servant . . . goe to such place . . . for trayneing or shall refuse to furnish such Servant . . . with sufficient Gunns and Ammunition he should pay a fine of fifty pounds of tobacco for each servant." [5] This fine was so small that many of the planters preferred paying it to fitting out the servant for war. The penalty was raised to 100 pounds of tobacco in 1678,[6] but the planters continued to evade the law whenever it was possible.

The servants were sometimes forced into miltary service before they reached the colonies at all. In the contest with the Dutch over the possession of New York, the British government practised gross deception upon servants bound for America and impressed them into their army. In 1673, Lord Culpepper proposed to the Council for Trade and Plantations a plan for reinforcing the British army in America. He advised that the commanders-in-chief of all vessels used for carrying planters and servants to Virginia and Maryland should be ordered to form into squadrons, and that the passengers be drilled for service. None were to be allowed to escape till the expedition was completed. The servants were to be told that they were bound for Maryland or Virginia until the vessels were well under way, and then resistance would be useless. Culpepper estimated that 600 or 800 servants annually embarked for those two colonies, "which would be a great reinforcement and cost little

---

[5] Arch. of Md. I. pp. 412-413.
[6] Ibid. VII. p. 54. Renewed in 1715 and 1719, Park's Laws, pp. 102, 109.

besides the ships themselves." The plan was recommended to the king and carried into effect.[7]

When the French and Indian War broke out, the old controversy over enlisting servants was renewed with vigor. The objections to the plan now assumed the proportions of an open revolt, the colonists denying the right of the governor or king to impair their contract with the servant by allowing or forcing him to join the army. Maryland at first considered this war as affecting the territorial claims of Virginia and Pennsylvania. She felt that the war did not immediately concern herself, and the Assembly maintained that nothing more could be expected of them than to send what available troops they had to assist the sister colonies and to provide defence in case the enemy later invaded Maryland. Although Governor Sharpe was anxious to raise both troops and money, as the crown had demanded, the people and the assemblymen refused to act, the latter stating that they were willing to resist an invasion of themselves or neighbors when they considered that necessity required it.[8] They consented to send delegates to the Albany convention, and appropriated £500 toward buying the good will of the Indians, but they rejected the plan of union by a unanimous vote in the lower house as "tending to the destruction of the rights and liberties of his Majesty's subjects in the province."[9]

After the capture of Washington at Little Meadow and the renewed depredations of the French and Indians on the frontiers of Maryland, Pennsylvania and Virginia, the Maryland Assembly at last considered means of defence *necessary*. On July 17, 1754, they voted £6000 to aid in repelling the invaders. To help raise this amount a duty was put on servants and convicts. The people were very much alarmed and a few companies of rangers had been raised before this

---
[7] Cal. State. Pap. Col. Nov. 13 and 15, 1673.
[8] McSherry, Hist. of Md. pp. 127-128.
[9] Ibid. 128-129.

act of the Assembly. The command of all the forces sent against the French on the Ohio was conferred by royal commission on Governor Sharpe of Maryland. Fort Cumberland was erected and later became a bone of contention between the governor and the people, who refused to furnish troops to defend it.

When the news of Braddock's overwhelming defeat reached Annapolis, Governor Sharpe set out for Frederick with a body of troops supported by private subscriptions of the panic-stricken citizens, who, at Annapolis, and even at Baltimore, began to fortify the towns. It was difficult, however, to get a sufficient number to leave their homes exposed and enter the ranks against the invaders.[10]

The foregoing will suffice to give an idea of the chaotic condition of military affairs in Maryland, when, in the early part of 1756, the king's recruiting officers entered that province to raise troops for the campaign against the French. The members of the Assembly thought only of guarding their own soverign rights and privileges from all encroachments from the neighboring colonies, their own governor, or the commander-in-chief of the army. Most freemen, either from indifference to the cause or from the danger of exposing their families to the ravages of the Indians, refused to enter the service. Under such conditions, the enlistment of the indentured servant who had no one but himself to care for was of great importance to the successful prosecution of the war. General Shirley, commander-in-chief of the American forces, at first forbade the enlisting of servants by recruiting officers. He continued this course, as he himself writes, "as long as the Circumstances of his Majesty's Service would admit. But this not now ye case."[11] It is impossible, he continues, to raise a sufficient number

---

[10] See McSherry, pp. 135-136.
[11] Shirley to Gov. Robt. H. Morris of Penn. Feb. 29, 1756, among MS. Cor. of Baltimore and officers of the Brit. Crown. Letter No. 13, Md. Hist. Soc. Library.

of troops without enlisting servants. He, therefore, revoked his former order and allowed the servants to join the ranks.

The recruiting of servants no sooner began than the masters prepared to resist it; first by protests, then by open violence. On February 2, 1756, Governor Sharpe wrote to General Shirley: "Within 3 or 4 days I have received several letters from the Magistrates in different Parts of this Province informing me that those of His Majesty's officers who have been ordered hither to recruit have lately received Your positive Instructions to enlist without Exception or Distinction all Apprentices and Servants, that they are persuaded to enter into the Service, that the Inhabitants having a great part of their Property vested in Servants unanimously oppose the Execution of such Instructions, & that unless their Cause of Complaint be speedily removed an Insurrection of the People is likely to ensue. The Magistrates as well as myself have & shall endeavor to prevent Mischief but as the officers are determined to persist I cannot promise that the people will be much longer restrained from expressing their Resentment by Actions: I think it my Duty to make this Representation to Your Excellency & hope you will not be averse to countermanding such orders otherwise I shall find myself under a Necessity of exercising the Power with which I am invested to preserve the peace of the province." [12]

This letter, coming from Governor Sharpe, who heartily supported the war, would not paint the case any darker than the facts warranted. The violence feared by the governor was not long in making its appearance. Robert Sterling, one of the recruiting officers, was apprehended and thrown into Kent county jail. From here, he wrote a letter to Governor Sharpe asking him to secure his release.[13] The local officers were shrewd enough to hold Sterling to answer an

---

[12] No. 9 Prop. Papers, Govs. Sharpe & Eden, Letter No. 27.
[13] Ibid. Letter No. 28.

action for damages, and the Council Board decided that the governor, as governor, could not discharge him.[14] Governor Sharpe was anxious to do everything in his power to relieve the recruiting officers. He appealed to the Attorney-General for his opinion on the right of the servant to enlist and on the right of the governor to discharge an action against a recruiting officer. He received the following reply, which agreed with the decision of the Council Board: (1) "I am of Opinion that a Master has a property in the labor of his Indented Servant for the time he has contracted to serve, and that he has no Right to enlist in his Majesty's Service Without his Master's Consent, untill the expiration of time of his servitude." (2) "I am of Opinion that a Recruiting Officer who enlists a Man's Indented Servant knowing him to be such is liable to the action of the Master, and that he ought to recover Damages adequate to the injury He sustains by the loss of his Servant, but if an officer should enlist a Servant not knowing him to be such I think no Action will lye against him, unless he should detain the Servant from his Master after he is informed of his being a Servant, In which case I think an Action would lye against him." (3) "I am of Opinion that the Governor cannot discharge any Civil Action commenced by a Man for the Recovery of his Property, and such is an Action commenced by a Master agst an Officer for taking his Servant out of his Service.

"22 March, 1756." [15]   "W. DORSEY.

The governor was powerless and could do nothing to relieve Sterling except to act on the advice of the Council and provide bail for the accused and order the Attorney-General to defend him in the next court.

Recruiting of servants continued and so also did the

---

[14] No. 9, Prop. Pap. Govs. Sharpe and Eden. Letter No. 30, March, 1756.
[15] No. 9, Prop. Pap. Govs. Sharpe and Eden. Letter No. 29, Md. Hist. Soc. Lib.

violence of the planters against the army officers. They were willing to expose the province to the ravages of the enemy, to defy the authority of king or governor rather than part with the servants whom they needed to cultivate the plantations. In August, 1756, Captain Gardner, in a letter to Governor Sharpe, complained that his recruiting sergeant had been attacked in July by Charles Ridgeley and a number of others. Six recruits were indentured servants. The planters threatened to whip the sergeant and his party out of town if he continued to enlist servants. Gardner appealed to the Attorney-General and the latter not only made light of, but even justified, the conduct of the planters.[16]

Disputes over enlisting servants, and sometimes armed resistance of the planters, continued all through the summer of 1756. The greatest obstacle to a satisfactory settlement of the controversy was that no one in the colonies, either officer or planter, knew enough about affairs in England to know whether or not the officers had any authority from Parliament to enlist servants. There were vague rumors that Parliament had pased some sort of an act at some time or another, but no one knew anything more about it. The planters denied the existence of such a law and were backed up in it by the local magistrates as well as the Attorney-General. Governor Sharpe, as late as August 21, speaks of an act which is "said to have been passed,"[17] and in a letter to Governor Morris, August 25, he asks if Morris has "seen or can get him a Copy of the Act of Parliament that is said to have been made to impower the Officers to enlist them (servants)."[18]

Washington and Governor Dinwiddie of Virginia had a very ludicrous misunderstanding over the rumored act, each accusing the other of stating that Parliament had passed

---

[16] Arch. of Md. VI. p. 461.
[17] Sharpe to Calvert, Arch. of Md. VI. p. 467.
[18] Sharpe to Morris, Arch. of Md. VI. p. 472.

a new law for recruiting servants. Washington was undoubtedly the one at fault. On August 4, 1756, he wrote to Dinwiddie stating that "There is an act of Parliament to allow all servants to enlist, and the owners to be paid a reasonable allowance for them." [19] On September 8, he wrote again in reply to a letter from Dinwiddie, "Your Honor's letter of the 19th mentions that I may enlist servants agreeable to the act of Parliament; but as I have not seen *that*, am at a loss how to proceed, until I receive your further orders or a copy of the act." [20] Dinwiddie, replying, September 13, accuses Washington of being the first to mention the act, "Sir, I mentioned in my Letter of the 9th Ult. to enlist Servants agreeable to the Act of Parliam^t; that act of Parliament I wrote from Y^r letter to me, I know of no Act of Parliam^t on that head." [21]

As a matter of fact there had been a law passed by Parliament in the spring of 1756, but neither Washington nor any one else in America knew anything of it when these discussions arose. The act was introduced in the Commons, March 17, 1756, and after several amendments, was finally passed in May.[22] It was enacted, the preamble states, to settle all "Doubts (which) may arise, whether such indented Servants can be legally enlisted." Power was given all the king's officers to enlist all servants who were willing to enroll, "any Law Custom or Usage to the contrary in any wise notwithstanding." But it was provided that in case the master should claim his servant within six months after he had enlisted, the officer in charge must either give him up or pay the master a reasonable compensation for the unexpired term of indenture.[23]

It was not definitely known in the colonies till fall

---

[19] Writings of Washington, Ford's Ed. I. p. 298.
[20] Ibid. p. 338.
[21] Hamilton's Letters to Washington, I. 364.
[22] Commons Journals.
[23] Eng. Stat. at Large, 29 Geo. II. Cap. 35, Secs. 1 and 2.

that Parliament had authorized the enlisting of servants, and the strife continued all through the summer. Another strife arose between the king's recruiting officers and the provincial officers. Washington complained to Governor Dinwiddie that unless power should be given by the Virginia Assembly to enlist servants that they would "all run off to the regular officers . . . and weaken our colony much."[24]

Unsuccessful attempts were made to induce the Assemblies of Maryland, Virginia, and Pennsylvania to appropriate money to pay the masters for the unexpired time of all servants who should enlist.

The king, through his Secretary of State, Henry Fox, sent a circular letter to the colonies ordering them to provide a compensation for masters whose servants should enlist.[25] The Maryland Assembly refused to comply with this order by more than a two-thirds majority[26] and made provision only for raising 300 men for the Royal American Regiment, allowing a bounty not exceeding five pounds for each man enlisting.[27] The Pennsylvania Assembly refused to make any provisions for defence unless the governor would accept a bill imposing a land tax for twenty years which were nine more than his powers would permit.[28] These refusals of the Assemblies to make adequate provisions for defence followed closely after the fall of Oswego,—a time when the French and Indians were making great inroads into the western parts of Pennsylvania and Maryland.

In spite of the opposition of the masters and the refusal of the Assemblies to vote a compensation for enlisted servants, the recruiting officers had to depend to a very great

---

[24] Writings of Washington, Ford's Ed. I. pp. 298, 300.
[25] Sharpe to Morris, Arch. of Md. VI. p. 472; Dinwiddie to Washington; Hamilton's Letters to Washington, I. pp. 364-365.
[26] Writings of Washington, Ford's Ed. I. p. 300, *note*.
[27] Arch of Md. VI. p. 497; Writings of Washington, I. p. 300, *note*.
[28] Sharpe to John Sharpe, Sept. 15, 1756, Arch. of Md. VI. p. 486.

extent on servants for filling up the ranks of the army. They secured more servants than freemen, the latter, as a rule, refusing to serve in any campaign outside of their own province. The servants, as a rule, were willing to enlist if their masters would let them, but most of the freemen could neither be persuaded nor forced to serve. For want of a draft law in Maryland, says Sharpe, it is "impossible to raise any Number of free Men in this Province," and "Few but Indented Servants have enlisted with the Recruiting Officers."[29] When the unexpired term of the servant was short the officers sometimes avoided trouble by purchasing the indenture from the master.[30]

The king's officers who had come to Maryland in the early part of the summer had enlisted so many servants that it was very hard for the provincial officers to secure recruits later. Governor Sharpe despaired of raising even the number voted by the reluctant Assembly.

Virginia had no better success in her efforts to induce or compel freemen to join the army. A law was passed in that colony imposing a fine of $10 upon freemen for refusing to serve when drafted. The freemen paid the fine and remained at home, leaving the army in as deplorable condition as ever.[31] Washington considers the only salvation of the army to be the passage of a law allowing the officers to impress servants. He urges that if such an act were passed the fines collected from the freemen would go a long way towards paying for the servants.[32] The servants were usually willing enough to enlist and many offered their services,[33] but as the legislatures neglected to appropriate money for paying the masters, many servants were prevented from serving.

---

[29] Sharpe to Calvert, Sept. 14, 1756, Arch. of Md. VI. p. 483.
[30] Sharpe to Morris, Ibid. p. 472.
[31] Dinwiddie to Washington, Aug. 19, 1756, in Letters to Washington, I. pp. 342-343; Writings of Washington, I. p. 299, *note* 1.
[32] Writings of Washington, I. p. 298.
[33] Ibid. p. 300.

Catholics and convicts, whenever they were known to be such, were excluded from the army. General Braddock was very much opposed to convicts, and forbade the officers to enlist them, but some found their way into the ranks. Whenever Governor Sharpe discovered that convicts had been enlisted, he replaced them by other recruits.

Very little is said in the records concerning the part played by servants in the Revolution. The first Assembly of the new State of Maryland which was held in February, 1777, passed an act for recruiting servants and apprentices, but it was repealed the same year.[34] They were enlisted in both Pennsylvania and Maryland, but there is no evidence that the number of this class of recruits was very large.

---

[34] Green's Laws of Md. 1777, Chaps. 3 and 10.

CHAPTER VIII.

Convicts.

Pike, in his History of Crime in England,[1] characterizes transportation of felons as "only an extension of the old law according to which persons who had taken sanctuary might abjure the realm." The old law referred to is an act passed in the reign of Elizabeth,[2] but this act does not appear to be the origin of the transportation of convicts to America nor the ground upon which it is based. The first transportation to America was based rather upon the royal order of King James I. than on Parliamentary legislation. Many persons who had been sentenced to death for various offences were granted royal pardon on condition of their being transported to some of the plantations.

The first act of Parliament which was passed for the purpose of sending offenders to America is the Act of Charles II., which provided for transporting Quakers to the plantations.[3] Another act was passed in the same reign [4] which gave power to judges at their discretion either to execute or transport to America for life the Moss-Troopers of Cumberland and Northumberland. Parliament, however, took very little interest in the matter, until the reigns of the Georges, when laws were made regulating transportation in detail. During these three reigns transportation of "his Majesty's seven-year passengers," as they were called, afforded a subject of frequent acts of legislation on both sides of the Atlantic.

From the reign of James I. till the separation of the colonies from England, large numbers of convicts were annually

---

[1] Vol. III. p. 109.
[2] 39 Eliz. Ch. 4.
[3] Stat. at Large 13 and 14. Charles II. Ch. 1, Sec. 2.
[4] Ibid. 18. Charles II. Ch. 3.

transported to the thirteen colonies, as well as the Barbadoes, Jamaica, and other islands, and influenced materially the history of both the mother country and the plantations. The English kings, ever solicitous about the want of laborers in America, kindly consented to send over all their unmanageable subjects to become servants in the plantations—a kindness not always appreciated by the colonists.

Convicts were sent to Virginia and Barbadoes before the founding of Maryland, but after the settlement of the latter colony, and continually throughout the colonial period, she received her share, and, in fact, a greater number than any other province. Colquohoun, who made a special study of crimes and criminals in England, in speaking of transportation after 1718, says: "This System continued for 56 years; during which period, and until the commencement of the American War in 1775, great numbers of Felons were sent chiefly to the Province of Maryland." [5]

Available material furnishes no clue to the actual number of convicts sent to Maryland before the Revolution. Scharf has estimated the number "at least twenty thousand," and the annual importation between the years 1750 and 1770, at "four to five hundred." [6] Judging from the newspaper records of the arrival of convicts at Annapolis and Baltimore, this estimate is not too high, if, indeed, it is high enough. Other estimates have been made of the whole number of "involuntary emigrants" sent from the British Isles to the American plantations. Between 1717 and 1775, the number sent from the Old Bailey alone is thought to be at least 10,000,[7] and the whole number from various places in Great Britain and Ireland at least 50,000.[8]

---

[5] A Treatise on the Police of the Metropolis, 6th Ed. p. 454.
[6] Hist. of Md. I. pp. 371-372. Pitkin gives the annual importation of convicts to Maryland as 300 or 400. Hist. of U. S. p. 113.
[7] Butler, British Convicts shipped to America,—Am. Hist. Rev. II. p. 25.
[8] Lang, Transportation and Colonization, pp. 37-38; Penny Cyclopaedia XXV. p. 138.

Transportation of felons simply on the order of the king, without parliamentary or other regulation, proved unsatisfactory, and it was recognized that some machinery ought to be provided for disposing of the large number condemned at every session of the courts. In June, 1661, a committee was appointed by the Council for Foreign Plantations "to consider of the best ways of encouraging and furnishing people for the Plantations, and how felons condemned to death for small offences and . . . sturdy beggars, may be disposed of for that use, and to consider an office of registry for same." [9]

For want of any regular system of transportation, pardoned felons very often had to undergo great hardships before they were sent to America. They were left in charge of the sheriffs to await the next jail delivery, without any provision being made for their support.[10] Both prisoners and sheriffs at various times petitioned the Council of State that power might be given the latter to speedily execute the order of transportation. Very often, security was required for the safe arrival of the convict in America and his non-appearance in England till his term of banishment had expired. Sir John Towers, who had been reprieved from a sentence of death in August, 1666, petitioned the king for a speedy transportation. He states that he has "long lain in a loathsome prison" because he was unable to furnish the necessary security for the fulfillment of the order of transportation. He begs the king to give authority to the sheriff to deliver him to the ship-captain without such security. After three months' delay, the request was granted.[11]

Without a license, the sheriffs were not allowed to deliver any felons to the transporters, and to secure such license they sometimes gave security themselves that any so de-

---
[9] Cal. St. Pap. June 3, 1661.
[10] Ibid. Dec. 19, 1662.
[11] Cal. St. Pap. Aug. and Oct. 15, 1666.

livered would not return to England till their term of banishment had expired. In this way they were relieved of the expense of supporting the convict.[12]

The committee appointed in 1661 to consider methods for transportation did nothing for three years; but, in 1664, a proposal was made to the king and council to constitute an office for "all vagrants, rogues, and idle persons that can give no account of themselves, felons who have the benefit of clergy, such as are convicted of petty larceny, vagabonds, gypsies, and loose persons, making resort to unlicensed brothels." They were to be transported from the nearest port and serve in the plantations four years, if over twenty years of age, and seven years, if under that age. In the proposed office an accurate register was to be kept of all persons transported, under penalty of £20.[13] In the same year the committee in their report recommend an act of Parliament as the only adequate remedy for the evils connected with transportation.[14] It was many years, however, before Parliament took any action, and what little was done to better the conditions was the work of the king and council. On September 14, 1664, the Lord Chancellor (Clarendon) was ordered to prepare letters-patent for the creation of the proposed office, which was put in charge of Roger Whitley. But as Parliament neglected to appropriate money to pay the salaries of responsible officers, the law failed to better the condition of the convict or to prevent persons from being kidnapped for transportation.[15]

The greatest number of the "seven-year passengers" sent to the plantations were ordinary criminals from various jails of Great Britain and Ireland. Among them were men and women of all ages and descriptions. They represented

---

[12] Cal. St. Pap. Col. Dec. 19, 1662.
[13] Cal. St. Pap. Col. 1664, No. 772. Another object of the office was to prevent spiriting.
[14] Ibid. 791.
[15] Kidnapping and the press-gang were evils to be feared by free men as well as bound servants or malefactors.

all crimes—if some of the offences may be so classed—from stealing a loaf of bread to sustain life, to highway robbery. The worst criminals were seldom transported, but were executed in large numbers after every session of the court.

The number was augmented at various times by the transportation of rebel convicts. Most of these were sent to the Barbadoes and other islands,[16] but during the eighteenth century some were sent to New England, Virginia, and Maryland. In the summer of 1717 one hundred and thirty-five Scotch rebels were sent to Maryland and sold as servants.[17]

It is difficult to tell, from the court records and state papers, where the greater number were sent, as there is seldom any more specific destination given than "the plantations" or "the West Indies"—which may mean any part of America. In the Calendar of State Papers for December 13, 1666, there is an interesting entry concerning the disposition of Scotch rebels. "The resolution about the Scotch rebels is to hang all ministers and officers; of the common sort one in ten is to be executed, one forced to confession and the rest sent to Plantations."

The rebels sent to the West Indies in the seventeenth century were required to serve ten years. In a letter of the king to the governor of Jamaica, he instructs the governor that all the late rebels sent to Jamaica "shall serve their masters ten years, without permission to redeem themselves by money or otherwise till that term be expired." The governor is ordered to propose a bill to the Council and Assembly for enforcing the order.[18] The term of servitude for the Monmouth rebels sent to Barbadoes was also ten years, while ordinary servants were bound for only four years.[19]

---

[16] See Hotten's Original List of Emigrants to America.
[17] See Scharf, Hist. of Md. I. pp. 385-389 for a full list and the proclamation of the Governor concerning them.
[18] Cal. St. Pap. Col. Oct. 11, 1685.
[19] Ibid. Lieut.-Gov. Stede to Lords of Trade, Feb. 3, 1686.

The Barbadoes won the approval of the king by their strict regulations for governing convict rebels,[20] which is doubtless the reason why so many more were sent there than elsewhere.

Even in the seventeenth century, when the demand for laborers was greatest, the planters were unable to appreciate the *kindness* of the English kings in making America a dumping-ground for their jail-birds and other objectionable subjects. As early as 1676, Maryland passed a law forbidding the importation of convicts into that province.[21] This law required every shipmaster on his entry into port to take an oath declaring whether any of the persons transported were convicts. If they were found to be felons, they were not permitted to be sold, given away, or in any otherwise disposed of. In order to land at all to dispose of the rest of his cargo, the master was required to give security that he would not dispose of the convicts, but remove them as soon as possible. Other persons were also forbidden to bring such felons to their plantations. All who should violate this law were liable to a fine of 2000 pounds of tobacco, one-half to the proprietor, the other to the informer. The crown lawyers declared the act void on the ground that it violated measures allowed and encouraged by Parliament. Nevertheless, it was continued at different times till 1692, when a new law was passed differing little from the former act.[22]

Objections were raised in other colonies about this time against the importation of felons, but apparently without avail. Virginia attempted to prevent the landing of convicts in December, 1678, but the king sent a peremptory order to the governor and other officers commanding them to permit Ralph Williamson "to land and dispose of fifty-two

---

[20] Cal. St. Pap. Col. May 10, 1686.
[21] Arch. of Md. II. pp. 540-541.
[22] Ibid. XIII. pp. 539-540; Scharf, Hist. of Md. I. p. 372; Bacon's Laws of Md.

convicted persons of Scotland, sentenced to be transported to our English plantations and such others as shall be convicted in Scotland, etc . . . without hinderance or molestation, any, law, order, or custom in Virginia to the contrary notwithstanding." [23]

Complaints against convict servants also came from the islands. John Style, writing from Jamaica to Secretary, Lord Arlington, July 24, 1665, asks why his Majesty does not send out a colony of free men "upon meate, drink, and wages," and not "your convicted gaol birds or riotous persons, rotten before they are sent forth and at best idle and only fit for the mines." [24]

But while the Americans protested against the intrusion of convicts into the plantations, the convicts were by no means anxious for the society of the colonists. Some of them preferred death to transportation, and refused to accept the latter alternative when the offer was renewed at the last moment.[25] From the accounts of America that were sometimes given by Englishmen, it is little wonder that the convicts chose death rather than servitude in the plantations.

Thus far, our attention has been confined to transportation in the seventeenth century. The eighteenth century, however, affords a greater and more interesting field for the study of convicts and their transportation. In this century Parliament assumed control and enacts definite laws for transporting felons. The colonists attempted by various measures to restrict or prohibit the objectionable traffic, but it continued in the middle colonies down to the Revolution. Maryland was especially the dumping-ground for English jails, and received more convicts than any other plantation on the continent. In 1776, Eddis writes that "Maryland is the only province into which convicts may be freely imported." [26] A contemporary, in 1767, estimates

---
[23] Cal. of St. Pap. Col. Dec. 17, 1678.
[24] Cal. St. Pap. Col.
[25] Stonyhurst MSS. quoted by Johnson. Foundation of Md., p. 25.
[26] Letters from America, p. 66.

the number imported into Maryland for the preceding thirty years at 600 per annum.[27]

The first act of the British Parliament concerning convicts was passed in the fourth year of King George the First "for the more effectual Transportation of Felons."[28] The preamble relates that punishment inflicted in England had ceased to prevent crime; that transportation by royal order had also proved a failure because the conditions were not always fulfilled; and that convicts were often allowed to escape to renew their crimes and meet a shameful and ignominious death. This much was true, but what followed concerning the desirability of these persons in America is more questionable. By this act, Parliament hoped to rid England of her objectionable inhabitants and *assist* the colonies by thrusting upon them a burden which England was unable to bear. The court which tried the prisoners was given full power to order the transportation of any persons convicted of crimes subject to the benefit of clergy. The term for this class of felons was fixed at seven years. This court or any succeeding court was given power to transfer such convicted persons to anyone who would contract to execute the sentence. Persons convicted of crimes without benefit of clergy could not be transported without special pardon of the king, and the term for these was fourteen years, or such term as the king might direct. Some of the worst offenders were banished for life. Persons contracting to transport convicts were given a property right in their service which might be disposed of at pleasure. They were also allowed a bounty for carrying the felons out of the realm.

The large number of persons convicted and the uncertainty of always being able to dispose of them while court was in session caused great suffering in the overcrowded

---

[27] Md. Gazette, July 30, 1767, extract in Williams, Hist. of the Negro Race in America, I. pp. 244-245.
[28] 4 Geo. I. Cap. 11, Stat. at Large.

prisons. This led to the passage of a law two years later which authorized the court to appoint two or more justices of the peace, who might dispose of the convicts as soon as the vessel reached port.[29]

The laws concerning convicts were not very well executed. Many of the felons escaped from the jails or returned before their term of banishment had expired. Still others escaped punishment because of the expense and trouble of their prosecution. To remedy this a reward of £20 was offered for the apprehension and conviction of all felons without benefit of clergy. Any convict returning before his term had expired was to suffer immediate death.[30] The Gentleman's Magazine gives a few cases where felons were executed for returning to England.[31]

The king by proclamation offered an additional reward of £100 for the conviction of robbers captured within five miles of London. This led some to make a regular business of prosecuting persons in order to obtain the reward, and many were convicted on manufactured evidence. In 1732, the Recorder of London petitioned the king to pay no more rewards unless at the request of the Lord Mayor or the judge who tried the felon because many innocent lives were "brought to Destruction by this most infamous practice."[32]

To make the return of convicts more difficult and to prevent ship-masters from making special arrangements with them or allowing them to escape, a new law was passed in 1747. The ship-master, under penalty of £50, was required to deliver to the custom officer at the port of landing a full list of all felons transported.[33] As copies of these were forwarded to the home government it was very easy to tell if any had escaped.

It was to the advantage of both transporter and convict

---

[29] 6 Geo. I. Cap. 23, Stat. at Large.
[30] 16 Geo. II. Cap. 15.
[31] Vol. 44, pp. 43, 493.
[32] London Magazine, I. p. 367.
[33] 20 Geo. II. Cap. 46.

to conceal the fact that the latter was one of "his Majesty's seven-year passengers." Although their term of servitude was longer than other servants, experience had taught the planters that they were hard to control and were liable at any moment to run away. They preferred other servants and would always pay a higher price for them. Besides, there had always been considerable opposition to convicts on moral grounds. The captains as far as possible represented their cargo to be respectable persons who wished to serve for their passage money, and very often the planters purchased convicts without knowing it.

Maryland as well as the British government attempted to frame laws which would prevent such deception in future. They did not, as in 1676, attempt to prohibit the importation of felons, but they endeavored to adopt measures which would enable the planters to know whether or not they were buying convicts and for what term they had been condemned to serve. The term of service was ever a source of dispute between masters and servants and unless the latter were proved to be convicts they were able to return to England at the end of four or five years.

In 1728, the Maryland Assembly enacted a law which required all ship-masters importing convicts into that province to bring a testimonial of the offence, the place of conviction and the number of years that each was required to serve. Violation of this law was punishable with a fine of five pounds for each convict not reported. The captain was required to declare upon oath whether any of his passengers were convicts, and a fine of five hundred pounds current money was imposed on all who refused to comply.[34]

Such regulations for the protection of the planters from the deception of the traders was as far as it was practicable for the Assembly to go. Any attempt to prohibit the importation of convicts was always combatted by the British

---

[34] Bacon's Laws of Md. 1728, Ch. 23.

officials. In 1723, Virginia had attempted to restrict importation by requiring the importer to give security of 100 pounds for the good behavior of each convict for a space of two months after he was disposed of to any planter in that province. The master was compelled to give security of ten pounds for the remainder of the term. Richard West, Chancellor of Ireland, in his opinion on this law, addressed to the Lords Commissioners of Trade, pronounced it a virtual prohibition of convicts and therefore contrary to the acts of Parliament. This measure, he thinks, would lead to a defeat of all British transportation laws.[35]

Transportation continued unabated in spite of all regulations made by the several colonies. The Gentleman's Magazine, the London Magazine, the Historical Register, and the Middlesex County Records all give accounts of the regular transportation from various part of England and Ireland. The jail deliveries, especially at Old Bailey, are given very regularly in these magazines, and there is hardly an issue that does not tell of a large number being sentenced to transportation in this court. Other courts are only occasionally mentioned, so it is impossible to compute with any degree of certainty the whole number transported. Their destination is equally difficult to ascertain. Usually, where it is mentioned at all, it is Virginia or Barbadoes, but in a few cases it is Maryland. These specifications may generally be taken to mean any part of America, as the British were not very particular when mentioning places in the Western Hemisphere. For example, at a court session in Middlesex county, twenty-four felons were ordered to be transported to "the island of Virginia or the islands called the Barbadoes or some other part of America (versus Virginie insulam seu insulas vocatas le Barbadoes aut aliquam aliam partem Americe) for seven years.[36]

---

[35] Chalmer's Opinions, pp. 437-438.
[36] Midd. Co. Rec. III. p. 337. Lord North at the time of the

The following are examples of many notices found in the magazines:

"430 rebel prisoners from the gaols of Carlisle, Lancaster, Chester, York, and Lincoln, were transported this month from Liverpool for the Plantations; 8 of them were drowned by a boat oversetting, not being able to swim, because handcuffed. This number with the rest makes about 1000 transported." [37]

"One hundred and five Felons convict, taken out of Newgate, the Marshalsea, and several other County Gaols, were put on Shipboard, to be transported to Maryland." [38]

"Felons transported from Newgate, May 17, 1736, 4 for life, 3 for 14 years, and 100 for 7 years." [39]

The Maryland Gazette records the arrival of many convict vessels all through the eighteenth century. Loads of 50 to 100 or more were regularly landed at the ports of Baltimore and Annapolis, especially the latter city. The editors of the day frequently indulged in jokes at the expense of this class of immigrants. For example, the Maryland Gazette gives the following account of the arrival of a convict ship at Annapolis:

"Friday last arrived here, from London, after a Passage of 29 Days, Capt. James Dobbins, in the Thames Frigate, with 130 of his Majesty's Passengers, who were at Home so expert and knowing in some *Arts*, that they were obliged to Travel for the *better peopling* of his Majesty's American Plantations, *at least for the Term of Seven Years.*"

But the newspapers do not give a complete record of the arrival of these vessels in Maryland. The advertisements for runaway convicts often state that they came at a particular time and in a particular ship, no account of which is given in the papers. Large, therefore, as the recorded numbers appear, the actual number was much greater.

Being unable to exclude convicts from Maryland, the Assembly, in July, 1754, passed a law which enabled them to

---

Revolution talks of the "Island of Virginia," Ed. Everett in N. A. Review, 1820, I. p. 345.
[37] Gent. Mag. May 31, 1747, XVII. & p. 246.
[38] The Hist. Reg. Vol. IV. Chron. Diary, p. 25.
[39] London. Mag. Vol. V.

derive some material benefit from their importation. A duty of twenty shillings was imposed on every convict brought into the province.[40] The object of this act was not prohibitory, but the duty was imposed to help raise £6000 provided in the same act for his Majesty's service in the defence of Virginia. The importers vigorously opposed the payment of the duty, and immediately set to work to secure the repeal of the law. Governor Sharpe was unwilling to have the act repealed, and urged that twenty shillings each on the large number of convicts imported would raise "a great part of the money that is to sink the £6000 that were granted by the act."[41] The matter was brought before the British Attorney-General, who pronounced the law contrary to the acts of Parliament, and threatened to proceed against the Maryland charter unless Baltimore dissented to the law.[42] Baltimore denied that the law was contrary to any act of Parliament, as the word *convict* did not appear in the Maryland act—they were called servants for seven years—and that as soon as they were landed in America they were no longer convicts, but servants by indenture or custom of the country.[43] This construction was finally accepted by the Attorney-General, and no further action was taken. The law was repealed in 1756 and the controversy ended.[44] As the number of convicts increased, public sentiment against their importation increased accordingly. A writer in the Maryland Gazette, July 30, 1767, evidently an importer, attempts to show that the great influx of convict servants is rather a benefit than a detriment to Maryland. He was answered by two inhabitants, who flatly deny that the people willingly receive them, but rather considered it one of their greatest misfortunes. By "representing," says

---

[40] Bacon's Laws of Md. 1754, Ch. 9.
[41] Arch. of Md. VI. p. 295. This is another testimony of the large number imported into Maryland.
[42] Ibid. 328.
[43] Ibid. p. 330.
[44] Bacon's Laws of Maryland, 1756, Ch. 5.

one of them, "that the general sense of the people is in favor of this vile importation, he is guilty of a most shameful misrepresentation and the grossest calumny upon the whole province. . . . Is this the way to purge ourselves from that false and bitter reproach, so commonly thrown upon us, *that we are the descendants of convicts?* As far as it has lain in my way to be acquainted with the general sentiments of the people on this subject, I solemnly declare, that the most discerning and judicious amongst them esteem it the greatest grievance imposed upon us by our mother country."[45] Virginia,[46] New York,[47] and Pennsylvania were equally indignant. Franklin, when told by the British officials that it was absolutely necessary to remove this class of persons by transportation, replied by asking if the same reason would justify the Americans in sending their rattlesnakes to England.[48]

Great Britain, nevertheless, continued to send her jail-birds to America in spite of all protests, and in 1768 [49] Parliament passed its last act for that purpose. The remonstrances of Franklin and other influential men produced some effect in 1770, and an attempt was made in the House of Commons to provide for sending criminals to Africa and the East Indies, instead of America. But the measure was defeated, largely through the opposition of Sir George Saville.[50]

The revolution finally accomplished what colonial legislation and remonstrance for over a century had failed to do. By 1779, Parliament came to the conclusion that transportation to the American colonies was "attended with many Difficulties," and it was provided that they might be "trans-

---

[45] Green's Gazette, Aug. 20, 1767.
[46] Va. Gazette, May 24, 1751. Quoted by Fiske, Old Virginia, II. 190, note 1.
[47] Independent Reflector in Smith's N. Y. pp. 319-320.
[48] Lang, Transportation and Colonization, p. 12.
[49] 8 Geo. III. Cap. 15.
[50] Hansard's Parl. Hist. XVI. p. 942.

ported to any Parts beyond the Seas, whether the same be situated in America or elsewhere." [51] The wording of the act thus left it lawful to resume transportation to America in case England should be successful in putting down her rebellious colonies. Unable to do this, she was forced to look elsewhere for a penal colony, and Australia soon became the recipient of the seven-year emigrants.

But the separation of the colonies from England did not entirely prevent adventurers from bringing over convicts to sell to the planters. The law of the first Congress for taxing the importation of certain persons" was intended to apply to convicts as well as slaves.[52] Some of the new states also passed laws against importing convicts. New Jersey, for example, fixed the penalty for each offence at $200 and costs.[53]

The immediate effect of the importation of felons was to considerably increase licentiousness and crime in the communities where they were purchased. The newspapers of the day show that most of the thefts and robberies were committed by runaway or freed convicts. But the permanent influence of the convict element on society in the colonies was comparatively small. The worst criminals were usually executed at home, and the majority of those transported were worthless and indolent, rather than vicious. The rigid discipline of the colonial laws and the experience acquired by seven years' hard labor converted the greater number of them into respectable and self-supporting citizens. The most depraved usually returned to England to renew their crimes "or withdrew from the haunts of civilization to lead half-savage lives in the backwoods." [54]

---

[51] Stat. at Large—19 Geo. III. Cap. 74.
[52] Madison Papers, III. 1428-30.
[53] Nixon's Digest, 3d. Ed. Laws of New Jersey, 1709-1861, p. 617.
[54] Fiske, Old Virginia and her Neighbors, II. pp. 188-189.

CONCLUSION.

Importation of servants into Maryland from Great Britain and Ireland seems to have reached its height about the middle of the eighteenth century. From that time down to the Revolution the number of voluntary servants brought into the colony gradually diminished. Convicts, on the other hand, came in ever-increasing numbers, and during the twenty years which preceded the Revolution, Maryland received nearly all that were transported. As slavery was firmly rooted in Virginia, there was little demand for convict labor, and laws were enacted to exclude them.[1] In Pennsylvania, the German immigrants more than supplied the demand for servants, and the convict element there was insignificant. But in Maryland the contractors always found a ready market for his Majesty's passengers, in spite of the sentiment against them.

After the convict trade was terminated by the Revolution, very few English-speaking servants came to the new state. Various travelers speak of the difficulty of obtaining white servants. Cooper,[2] who traveled in Maryland in 1793, says that it is impossible to procure any servants "but Negroslaves." Two years later, Weld[3] writes that "it is a matter of the utmost difficulty to procure domestic servants of any description." These remarks apply only to English and Irish servants, as the Germans and Swiss at that time were seldom purchased for domestics.

The falling off in the number of servants from Great Britain and Ireland was due to several causes. None now found it necessary to emigrate on account of religious persecu-

---

[1] Eddis Letters, p. 66.
[2] Some Information respecting America, p. 20.
[3] Travels in the United States, p. 29.

tion. The social and economic conditions at home were much better than in the preceding centuries, and a greater proportion of the immigrants were able to pay for their transportation. Modern improvements had shortened the voyage and greatly reduced its cost.

Another thing which tended to reduce the number imported was the stigma which attached to the institution. So many convicts were annually sent to expiate their crimes by servitude in the plantations that America came to be looked upon as a sort of penal colony, and those who were unable to pay their way preferred to remain at home rather than to cast their lot with the seven-year passengers from Old Bailey and Newgate. This impression was encouraged by the British officials and writers whose desire it was to discourage emigration.

The servant trade was entirely stopped by the war, and it was never revived with any great vigor.[4] Now that America had become a separate state, still greater efforts were made to restrain British subjects from going there. Writers never tired of depicting the new republic as a land of barbarism and wretchedness. Lord Sheffield, writing in 1784, represents emigration as the resource only for the culprit and of those who have made themselves the objects of contempt. "It is generally calculated that not above one emigrant in five succeeds so as to settle a family. . . . Irishmen just emancipated in Europe, go to America, to become slaves to a negro. . . . The better sort of emigrants are begging about the streets."[5] The British reviews were equally zealous in their denunciations of America and their warnings to emigrants.[6]

But what was more effectual still in reducing the number of servant immigrants was the restriction put upon emigra-

---

[4] Hildreth, IV. p. 93.
[5] Observations on the Commerce of the American States, pp. 193, 196.
[6] See Walsh's Appeal, Secs. VII. and VIII.

tion to America by the British government. In 1794, the emigration of all skilled laborers was prohibited. By the navigation law of 1817, vessels bound for the United States were permitted to carry but one passenger for every five tons of the vessel, while those going to other countries were allowed to carry twice that number.[7] With these regulations in force, no contractor could profitably transport servants to America.

The German and Swiss redemptioners continued to come in large numbers long after the Revolution. There was no appreciable falling off in the number till after the year 1817. The records for that year, given in Niles' Register, show that the emigration from both Germany and Switzerland was very large. May 24, fourteen vessels are reported as preparing at Amsterdam to bring 5000 emigrants to the United States. From the first to the sixteenth of May, 5817 emigrants passed Mayence on the way to America.[8] It was estimated that the number of Germans who left Baden for America during the summer of 1817 was 18,000.[9] The proportion of servants cannot be safely affirmed.

But in the years 1817 and 1819, measures were adopted on both sides of the Atlantic which dealt a death blow to the institution of servitude by rendering it unprofitable for contractors to longer engage in the traffic. In 1817, steps were taken in both Holland and Switzerland to investigate the condition of emigration and to prevent the passengers from being crowded in ships by contractors and carried to America. Switzerland refused to grant passports to the United States to any emigrant who was unable to present a bill of exchange of at least 200 florins payable at Amsterdam.[10] This practically prohibited the emigration of all who were unable to pay for their transportation. Holland

---

[7] See Walsh's Appeal, Secs. VII. and VIII.
[8] Niles' Register, July 19, 1817, p. 333.
[9] Niles' Register, Aug. 16, 1817, p. 397.
[10] Ibid. Aug. 2, 1817, XII. p. 365.

also sent out an ambassador to study the emigration problem and to devise remedies for protecting the emigrants. These regulations did much to reduce the number of emigrants who found it necessary to bind themselves into servitude when they reached America.

While these restrictions were being put upon emigration by the European governments, laws were enacted in the United States which were still more effectual in bringing the institution to an end. The German Society of Maryland, which was incorporated in 1817, set vigorously to work to purge the system of the abuses which had long been practiced upon the poor and ignorant redemptioners. They secured the passage of a law which compelled ship-masters to provide wholesome food for the immigrants and to care for the sick at their own expense. No person could be held to pay for the passage of a deceased relative or friend no matter what contract had been previously made. The term of servitude was reduced to four years. Armed with this law the society at once set to work to strictly enforce its provisions and to bring offenders to justice. It was soon found, however, that state laws did not have adequate jurisdiction in dealing with foreign ships and the matter was laid before Congress. In March, 1819, Congress passed a law which limited the number of passengers to two for every five tons of the vessel. A penalty of $150 was imposed for every passenger that was carried in excess of that number, and if the excess amounted to twenty passengers the vessel was forfeited to the United States.

Official reports show a remarkable falling off in the number of German immigrants after the passage of these laws. From October 1, 1819, to September 30, 1820, the whole number of German and Swiss immigrants landing at Baltimore was only 299, while only 20 came to Philadelphia during the same period.[11]

---

[11] Report of the Secretary of State, Washington, Feb. 1821.

Indenture of white servants in Maryland practically ceased at this time. There is no entry relating to redemptioners in the books of the German Society after September, 1819.[12] Private individuals continued to import persons under such a contract for a few years longer and isolated cases are mentioned as late as 1835, but the number is insignificant.

For nearly two centuries white servitude played a very important part in the industrial history of Maryland. Employed at first as a means of building up a landed aristocracy, it developed later into an institution approaching in some respects chattel slavery. Its efficiency as a system of labor in colonial days was far superior to either free labor or negro slavery. No other system could have supplied a sufficient number of laborers at so little cost to the planters. The long and certain term of service made it possible for planters to profitably cultivate extensive plantations and build up a lucrative foreign trade. It supplied the colony not only with agricultural laborers, but with tradesmen and professional men. Its superiority over negro slavery retarded the growth of that institution.

In general, the effect of this system of labor on the servant himself was beneficial. Five years' experience under the rule of an exacting master converted many an indolent immigrant into an industrious and prosperous citizen.

As a means of promoting emigration, this sustem was equally successful. It afforded relief to thousands of the oppressed and starving peasants of Europe by providing a way of reaching America without paying for their passage in advance. By drawing off the superfluous population of Europe it did more to lessen pauperism and crime than all the laws on the statute books.

But the time came when this stimulus to emigration was no longer necessary. The social and economic conditions which had called the system into existence had passed away,

---

[12] Hennighausen, Redemptioners, p. 21.

and its continuance was of interest only to those who were engaged in the transportation. The abuses practiced by these dealers in men at last became so flagrant that public opinion was aroused against the institution and measures were adopted which brought it to an end.

Index

A
Arlington
  Lord, 98
Arundel
  Lord, 12

B
Bacon
  Nathaniel, 53
Baltimore
  Lord, 10, 11, 21, 30, 68
Benton
  Mark, 63
Billsbury
  Henry, 63
Bird
  Simon, 63
Boehme
  Charles, 39
Bowles
  Edward, 25
Braddock
  General, 91
Brays
  James, 39
Butler, 68
  Mary, 68, 69
  William, 68

C
Calvert
  Charles, 21, 26
  Leonard, 13, 19, 63
Carey
  Thomas, 21
Charles II, 92
Claiborne
  William, 53
Claibourne, 61
Clarendon
  Lord, 95

Clobery, 61
Cook
  Eben, 72
Cooper, 107
Copley
  Thomas, 43
Cornwallis
  Captain, 21, 61
Culpepper
  Lord, 82

D
Danby
  John, 65
Danker, 73
Dinwiddie
  Governor, 87, 88, 89
Dobbins
  James, 103
Dorsey
  W., 86
Drake
  William, 64
Dulany
  Daniel, 79

E
Eddis, 32
Edwards
  Joseph, 25
Elizabeth I, 7, 92
Evelin, 61
  Captain, 20

F
Fearon, 32
Fenwick
  Cuthbert, 24, 61
Fisher
  Edward, 40
Fox
  Henry, 89

Frizell
  Susan, 58

G
Gardner
  Captain, 87
Gilbert
  Humphrey, 8
Gordon
  Christian, 46
Greene
  Thomas, 41
Guest
  Walter, 40

H
Hardman
  Daniel, 51
Harrington
  William, 63
Harris
  Mary, 43
Harvey
  Nicholas, 24
Hawley
  Gabriel, 12
Hoy
  Adam, 39

I
Ireland
  William, 64
Irish Nell, 68

J
James I, 8, 9, 92
Jarbo
  John, 81
Jones
  Robert, 25

L
Lewger
  Ann, 20

John, 20, 41
Little
   John, 63
Lyon
   Mathew, 79

M

Mathews
   Hannah, 41
Mittleberger, 32
Monmouth
   Duke, 96
Moore
   Thomas, 41
Morgan
   Captain, 64
   Henry, 63
Morris
   Governor, 87
Muhlenberg, 32

N

Naunton
   Secretary, 9
Norman
   John, 25
Nunn
   John, 25

P

Peckham
   George, 8
Penruddock
   Anthony, 21

Q

Quigley
   Patrick, 51

R

Ridgeley
   Charles, 87
Robinson
   Edward, 21

Rowley, 33

S

Sandys
   Edwin, 9
Saville
   George, 105
Sharpe
   Governor, 30,
     31, 33, 42,
     83, 84, 85,
     86, 87, 90,
     91, 104
   John, 33
Sheffield
   Lord, 108
Shirley
   General, 84, 85
Sluyter, 73
Sly
   Gerard, 19
   Robert, 19
Spink
   Henry, 24
Sterling
   Robert, 85, 86
Stone
   Governor, 12,
     16, 18
Style
   John, 98
Sullivan
   General, 79

T

Talbott
   George, 21
Taylor
   George, 79
   Robert, 63
Thompson
   William, 81
Thomson
   Charles, 79

Thornton
   Matthew, 79
Todd
   Thomas, 41
Towers
   John, 94
Turner
   Arthur, 25

V

Vaughan
   Robert, 63
Verdeen
   Alexander, 42

W

Ward
   Thomas, 58, 65
Washington, 87, 88,
   89, 90
Weest
   Thomas, 63
Weld, 107
Wells
   John, 64
   Richard, 58
West
   Richard, 102
Weston
   Thomas, 20
Whitley
   Roger, 95
Wickes
   Joseph, 46
Williamson
   Ralph, 97
Wilson
   James, 65
Windebanke, 12
Winthrop, 33
Wright
   Frances, 76

www.ingramcontent.com/pod-product-compliance
Lightning Source LLC
Chambersburg PA
CBHW070531100426
42743CB00010B/2045